Christianity is not a religion aimed at swallowing up the individual into the essence of God as the rivers are lost in the sea. To the contrary, self-realization harmonizes with the teaching of the Bible much better than self-abnegation does, so why should we hesitate to say so?

a true view of YOU

Stanley C. Baldwin

Regal Books
A Division of GL Publications
Ventura, CA U.S.A.

Other good reading:

Do I Have to Be Me? by Lloyd H. Ahlem
Reaching Your Possibilities Through Commitment by Gerald W. Marshall
Can You Love Yourself? by Jo Berry

The foreign language publishing of all Regal Books is under the direction of Gospel Literature International (GLINT). GLINT provides financial and technical help for the adaptation, translation, and publishing of books for millions of people worldwide. For information regarding translation, contact: GLINT, P.O. Box 6688, Ventura, California 93006.

Published by Regal Books
A Division of GL Publications
Ventura, California 93006
Printed in U.S.A.

Library of Congress Cataloging in Publication Data

Baldwin, Stanley C.
A true view of you.

Includes bibliographical references.
1. Conduct of life. I. Title.
BJ1581.2.B323 248.4 81-84569
ISBN 0-8307-0779-4 AACR2

To
Kathy Holland
Krystal Brown
Karen Kraus
my little sweethearts,
now grown-up women of God.

CONTENTS

Introduction

"This could confuse some of our people," a pastor told me, referring to my seminar flyer. "We have been teaching them for years to renounce self, that the self-life is base and sinful. Now you want to tell them how to 'like themselves, free themselves and develop their potential.' You should avoid that kind of language because it smacks of humanism and runs counter to the biblical description of man."

I was somewhat intimidated. I knew the problem existed, but had felt that people simply needed to be reeducated a bit. They needed to understand that the self is not essentially evil, though the word has sometimes carried that connotation. But now I was wondering. If the Bible consistently uses the term in a negative sense . . .

When I got home, I dug out my *Young's Concordance*. Did I get an education! I discovered that the Bible does not use the word *self* in the negative way the pastor said it did. The Bible does not talk about *self* as an entity in the way it sometimes talks about *the flesh*—as the unregenerate, base element in man. Self is mostly used in a morally neutral sense as in the reflexive pronouns (myself, himself, yourself). The few exceptions to this usage are in passages such as Titus 1:7 and 2 Peter 2:10, where Scripture warns against being self-willed, otherwise translated headstrong, overbearing, or arrogant.

If, then, Christian people have a negative concept of the word *self*, it is because they have been mistaught. It is time for those who have mistakenly made *self* synonymous with *the flesh* to correct their error.

Apart from the connotations of the word *self*, however, Christians are properly concerned about an overemphasis on man, his needs and the fulfillment of those needs. About narcissism; man tends to be egocentric anyhow, that is his basic sin—he is self-centered instead of God-centered; too much talk about a good self-image, freeing oneself, developing one's potential may simply cater to man's egocentric bent; God and Christ should be kept central in our teaching and in our thinking.

The truth is, however, that Christianity concerns both God and man. Healthy and correct concepts about both are essential. One can become unbalanced even in focusing on God, as the following sometimes-popular poem illustrates:

Oh, the bitter pain and sorrow
That a time could never be
When I proudly said to Jesus,
"All of self, and none of Thee."

Yet He found me; I beheld Him

Bleeding on th' accursed tree;
And my wistful heart said faintly,
"Some of self, and some of Thee."

Day by day His tender mercy,
Healing, helping, full and free,
Brought me lower, while I whispered,
"Less of self, and more of Thee!"

Higher than the highest heavens,
Deeper than the deepest sea,
"Lord, Thy love at last has conquered;
None of self and all of Thee!"
—Theodore Monod

The poem, while it is beautifully reflective of a growing consecration, has problems. First, it uses the word *self* in a negative, contrary-to-God sense, typical of some Christians but not typical of Scripture. Second, if taken literally, it urges an extreme renunciation of the self more consistent with Hindu theology than with Christianity. If Monod's final prayer were actually granted, there would be no personage left to glorify or enjoy God.

Actually, those who shrink from a positive use of the word *self* are not all that God-centered. Even their evangelism is usually ego-centered. They seldom urge people to be born again in order to glorify God. No, they tell people it's either be converted or be lost. The very expression *saved* is man-centered. After all, it's not God who is being saved; it is man. I am in no way deprecating the salvation message. I'm only pointing out the self-interest upon which it is based.

Christian music reflects this same self-interest. I grew up in a fundamentalist church. Self was equivalent to sin. Nevertheless, our leaders taught us to sing heartily:

> If you want joy, real joy, wonderful joy;
> Let Jesus come into your heart.[1]

It's hard to imagine a more unabashed appeal to self-interest. There's no concern here for the glory of God. No ethical or moral principle is advanced. It's plainly and simply advice on how to get the joy you want, through Jesus.

That chorus was not exceptional. The music of the church probably appeals to self-interest more often than not.

"What a Friend We Have in Jesus!" Why is He such a good friend? "All our sins and griefs to bear!"

"Trust and Obey." Why? "For there's no other way *to be happy* in Jesus."

"Rock of Ages." What about it? "Let me hide myself in Thee."

"The Old Rugged Cross." Ah, at last, a song centering on the redemptive work of our Lord Jesus Christ. Yes, but even here, we end up singing, "I will cling to the old rugged cross, and *exchange it someday for a crown*."

Don't misunderstand. I'm not finding fault with the songs. I'm only pointing out that Christianity is not anti-self, and that we ought not to reject psychological teaching consistent with Scripture simply because we have an unfounded emotional reaction against the term *self* or because we imagine the best Christianity to be selfless.

Otherwise we had better rewrite the hymns of the church. But that would not solve the self-interest problem, for, as it turns out, even the Bible appeals to us on that level.

"Believe in the Lord Jesus." Why? "And you will be saved" (Acts 16:31).

"Do not judge." Why? "Or you too will be judged" (Matt. 7:1).

Jesus said to one man, "If you want to be perfect, go, sell your possessions and give to the poor, and *you will have treasure in heaven*" (Matt. 19:21, italics added).

"Let us not become weary in doing good." Why? Just because doing good is the Christian way to live? No, "for at the proper time *we will reap* a harvest if we do not give up" (Gal. 6:9, italics added).

One last example: "Do not let this Book of the Law depart from your mouth; meditate on it day and night, so that you may be careful to do everything written in it. Then *you will be prosperous, and successful*" (Josh. 1:8, italics added).

Christianity is not a religion aimed at swallowing up the individual into the essence of God as the rivers are lost in the sea. To the contrary, self-realization harmonizes with the teaching of the Bible much better than self-abnegation does, so why should we hesitate to say so?

What is the Bible all about then? What is the nature of Christianity? If we say it is about God and His glory we are right but we have not said enough. If we say the Bible is about man and his needs we are also right but we have certainly not said enough. It is about man as a creature of God and his needs as they are met by God's loving providence. It is about God as He can be known and loved and served by man.

Humanism, on the other hand, is "a philosophy that asserts the dignity and worth of man and his capacity for self-realization through reason and that often rejects supernaturalism" (Webster).

If we urge people to find self-realization through responding to God, we certainly are not embracing a humanism that "rejects supernaturalism." We may be promoting a sort of "theistic humanism," I suppose, but if we are, then so does the Bible.

With these thoughts in mind, I offer to the community of believers—and to any others who may come across it—this book. I am not a psychologist so I do not write from that particular professional viewpoint. What I mean to do, and have done, is to apply the principles of Scripture to some of the psychological teachings of our day—and, even more so, to the human condition as I observe it. Particularly, I have applied biblical principles to the question of how we should see ourselves.

If I seem to have come down on a positive, self-realization note, so much the better. I am not likely to promise more in this regard than the Scripture warrants. How could I when "all things are yours, whether Paul or Apollos or Cephas or the world or life or death or the present or the future—all are yours, and you are of Christ, and Christ is of God" (1 Cor. 3:21-23)?

Note

1. "If You Want Joy" by Joseph D. Carlson.

PART I
A True View of You

Chapter 1

Because You Laugh, Should I Feel Funny?

I have a certain pair of shoes that are tricky to walk in. The soles are corrugated and are thicker at the instep than anywhere else. Ordinarily I can walk fine in them, but occasionally if I am in a hurry that thick instep trips me up and I have to be fast on my feet to keep from falling.

I was all dressed up one day and crossing an intersection in the city of Salem, Oregon, on my way to visit a pastor about some meetings in his church. Right in the middle of the intersection as I was hurrying to make the light, my shoes did their thing to me. I was not nimble enough to recover this time, and down I went.

Talk about embarrassed! You'd have thought I had done something shameful the way I scrambled to my feet and avoided looking around at anyone who might be watching. I quickly brushed myself off and hurried on as though nothing had happened, ignoring the painful bruise on my elbow that I surely would have stopped to examine had I been in private.

Why did I behave that way? Certainly I had done nothing of which to be ashamed.

Though I didn't try to analyze my feelings at the time, it is clear on reflection that my distress—like all embarrassment, no doubt—was due to viewing myself from another's perspective. I was an object of amusement, a spectacle to be laughed at, a clumsy oaf.

Now, why do I tell you this? First, you deserve to know that though I have often spoken and now write about how to have a healthy self-image, I am not immune to the negative influence of others myself. Accordingly, you will find here no easy, once-for-all solutions to the problem. Instead, we will explore solid biblical principles that work for me when I apply them and that can be expected to work for you as well.

Second, I recount the tricky-shoe episode because although it was a trivial incident, analyzing the nature of embarrassment is not so trivial.

Embarrassment reflects the fact that our view of ourselves is influenced by others' views of us. People frequently affect the way we think about ourselves, and even when they fall short of that, they can still affect how we feel.

Longshoreman philosopher Eric Hoffer expressed the concept as follows: "It is thus with most of us: we are what other people say we are. We know ourselves chiefly by hearsay."

When people give us negative feedback we tend to internalize that and think or feel badly about ourselves. When they affirm us we feel good and inwardly applaud ourselves.

My embarrassment over the falling incident illustrates the operation of negative feedback. For an example of the positive variety, consider the Special Olympics, a nationwide program of athletic events for retarded people.

Every entrant in the Special Olympics is awarded a ribbon, regardless of how he or she places in the competition. Each is also greeted at the finish line by "huggers and back-slappers" who praise the person's efforts to the cheering of the crowd.

The result is smiles and shining eyes, the proud wearing of ribbons, joy on the faces and in the hearts of the athletes.

Why?

Not because they have outdone someone else, but because they see themselves through the eyes of others as deserving of praise and recognition.

Some literature, both in philosophy and psychology, maintains that *all* self-awareness depends upon and is created by our interaction with others. While that could be debated, much of our self-concept seems clearly conditioned by such feedback.

Damaging Distortions

The difficulty with this feedback system of self-evaluation is that it subjects us to great distortions of reality in the way we see ourselves. Three major distortion factors are at work.

First, others do not always perceive us correctly. They often misunderstand our actions, misread our intent. Seeing our shyness as aloofness, they may call us proud. Reading our eagerness as arrogance, they may try to cut us down to size. Then, too, others have emotional needs and problems of their own which may lead them to judge us unjustly.

Second, we may misinterpret what others say and do. For example, if we are over-sensitive any correction or criticism may be taken as a personal insult, a message that we are not acceptable.

Third, the values by which we are rated may be far astray from the mark. One cannot live uprightly in this perverse world without being put down for it by someone. As the Scripture says, "They think it strange that you do not plunge with them into the same flood of dissipation, and they heap abuse on you" (1 Pet. 4:4).

Sometimes the world's distorted evaluation of us is apparent, as was the case with my shame over tripping in public. Intellectually I knew that falling down was nothing against me. Even so, I was shaken emotionally almost as much as if I had performed a shameful act.

What would be one's trauma, then, if both intellectually and emotionally one accepted a distorted view from the world? One could be severely damaged.

Jill was 11 years old and slightly plump when a teacher at school commented about her roly-poly shape. At home that night, Jill's mirror told her the teacher was right—even too kind. She was worse than chubby, she told herself. She was ugly fat.

The horror of her condition burned itself into Jill's mind. She began to eat less but without immediate effect, of course. The image staring back at her from the mirror still looked repulsive. Soon her excess flesh became an obsession to Jill.

Today, at age 16, Jill weighs 87 pounds and is diagnosed as suffering from *anorexia nervosa*, a mental illness marked by loss of appetite and, in advanced stages, by the inability to keep food down. It is a condition that can actually lead to death by starvation. While Jill's disease cannot be specifically attributed to her neurosis about being overweight, one might certainly suspect a connection.

No rational appeal to Jill can help her. Just as I knew I had done nothing shameful when I fell in public, Jill "knows" she is not overweight. And just as my knowledge did not keep me from feeling embarrassed, Jill's does not keep her from feeling as if she is ugly fat.

In a thousand subtle and not-so-subtle ways, people are being damaged today by the world's distorted views of them. To expose many of these errors, and to counteract them, is the purpose of this book.

How Can We Get an Undistorted View of Ourselves

A familiar and oft-quoted verse of Scripture says, "Do not conform any longer to the pattern of this world, but be transformed by the renewing of your mind" (Rom. 12:2). This principle is appropriately applied to many areas of the Christian life. What most of us fail to realize is that it applies in its immediate context to the issue raised here—namely, the need to see ourselves correctly instead of as the world sees us.

Observe. Immediately after telling us not to conform to the world but to be transformed by a renewed mind the Scripture says: "For by the grace given to me I say to every one of you: Do not think of yourself more highly than you ought, but rather think of yourself with sober judgment, in accordance with the measure of faith God has given you" (Rom. 12:3).

What is the subject under discussion? How we are to think of ourselves.

We need to make one critical preliminary observation at this point. According to this Scripture it is not only permissible but desirable to "think of yourself."

Some say otherwise. Some tell us we must forget ourselves; we must not think of ourselves at all. Such teaching is an understandable reaction to the "me first" or "me only" attitude characteristic of much of the present generation. It is also an accepted, traditional way of thinking in evangelical circles.

However, it does not square with Scripture. The Bible does not say: "Do not think of yourselves more highly than you ought *but rather forget yourself.*" No, it says: "Do not think of yourself more highly than you ought, but rather think of yourself with sober judgment."

Certainly, to be preoccupied always with thoughts of ourselves is not healthy. On the other hand, some kind of self-concept is not only proper but inescapable. As self-conscious beings, aware of our own existence, we cannot help having some underlying assumptions about ourselves.

It is critically important that our underlying assumptions be correct because virtually everything we do or say flows from what we are or think ourselves to be.

Scripture says our self-concept should be based on "sober judgment." The word *sober* here could be translated "sound-minded" or "sane." We are called then to a sane self-evaluation.

What is likely to be the case instead? We are likely to be unsound in our self-evaluation, too much influenced by the world.

Now, when we are told not to be conformed to the world in this area, we are assigned quite a task inasmuch as, ordinarily, virtually all self-evaluation originates from one's interaction with others. We, by contrast, are told to be transformed by a renewed mind, which is to say that our self-concept must originate from God and His Word and from His Spirit dwelling within us, not from the world.

That is an absolutely profound difference, but doing what God says here is not necessarily all that difficult. Many Christians can testify that just such a thing is happening in their lives. Though they have at times been saddled with a world-conditioned view of themselves, the Spirit of God has used the Word of God to transform their thinking—and as a result, their lives.

Jerry Cook's experience is perhaps quite typical. He writes:

> I lived a lot of my life trying to get God to accept me. I didn't like me very well. I was too short. My ears were too big. I wasn't put together the way I thought best.
>
> I was crossing the street in Seattle one day when the Lord spoke to me clearly, "Jerry, why don't you quit trying to be a Christian? You are one. You are accepted in the Beloved." I did not even know that last phrase was in the Bible.
>
> Three days later, I was lying on my bed in the room I was renting near the college. I opened my Bible to Ephesians, chapter 1, and began reading. When I reached the sixth verse, it jumped on me

> like a thing alive—I am "accepted in the beloved" (*KJV*).
>
> That experience totally changed my life. Suddenly I wasn't trying to get God to like me anymore. He had liked me all the time.[1]

So far we have said three important things.

1. Ordinarily our self-concept is largely if not altogether determined by the attitude of others (our world) toward us.
2. The world's judgments of us are not reliable and are often wrong.
3. A new, correct, and liberating way of thinking about ourselves can come to us from God.

In succeeding chapters we will observe some of the many ways these principles work in our lives.

Note

1. Jerry Cook with Stanley C. Baldwin, *Love, Acceptance and Forgiveness* (Ventura, CA: Regal Books, 1979), p. 88.

Chapter 2

A Loaf of Barley Bread

I was in the city of Eugene, Oregon, conducting a "Take Charge of Your Life" seminar on how to "like yourself, free yourself, and develop your potential." A young man approached me halfway through. "What you say is all well and good," he remarked, "for those who have lots of potential but a low self-image. But some of us don't just *feel* inferior; we *are* inferior."

If you are like that young man you desperately need to hear what God has to say on this subject, because the natural human inclination is to get things all out of balance one way or another.

Sober judgment—sane self-evaluation—requires that we see our limitations, our weaknesses, our failings as well as our strengths. Both are a part of the true picture.

There was a day when the churches sounded forth loud and clear about the dangers of pride. Some still do. People must be kept from thinking too highly of themselves.

Today in many churches, however, the pendulum has swung to the opposite extreme. The teaching is geared totally toward building self-esteem. People must be kept from thinking too lowly of themselves.

Some teaching goes even further. It says that we are such wonderful people that we can do anything we set our minds to. All we need is the faith and courage to venture out and God will surely bring us through to glorious and wonderful triumph. Perhaps few say that in so many words, but that is what is sometimes heard.

Such was the case with the "truly inferior" young man in Eugene who had a heartrending story to tell. As a result of hearing various positive thinking, you-can-do-whatever-you-set-your-mind-on, human potential presentations, he confidently launched into a business he had wanted to pursue. When things didn't work out he ran through the litany again: keep faith, don't give up, you can do it if you believe you can.

The young man stubbornly pursued his dream, sacrificing everything to it, until his wife took their children and left him. He became hopelessly in debt, and the business dwindled to nothing.

Now I was seeing him a couple of years later. He was working at a menial job, had remarried, and was beginning to fellowship with God's people again. He was also wounded and scarred. He felt he had been misled by those who encouraged him to assume that anyone has what it takes to achieve his dreams if he but believes in himself.

"Remember," he told me, "some of us don't just feel inferior; we *are* inferior."

If you feel inferior or if you "are inferior," you need to consider four important facts about inferiority. And, please, don't tune out until you've considered all four, because the first points, while valid, may be the weakest in terms of actually helping you.

1. Everyone Is Inferior in Some Ways

Ludwig von Beethoven had a pockmarked face and his front teeth protruded. His hair was unruly, and he looked like he was always scowling. His mother died when he was 16, and his father was a drunk. Ludwig himself had a violent temper and was a poor manager of money. Worst of all for a musician and composer, he began going deaf at age 30. Yet he was one of the greatest composers of all time, with much of his best work being done after he had totally lost his hearing.

The apostle Paul was personally unattractive. People said his bodily presence was "unimpressive" and his speech contemptible (see 2 Cor. 10:10). Not very promising traits for a preacher. Yet Paul changed the history of the world through his preaching and his writing.

Napoleon was a little sawed-off runt so short that even his friends called him the "Little Corporal."

Abraham Lincoln was physically ugly, with a tall, gangly build, a big nose, and a wart on his craggy face.

Franklin D. Roosevelt was a cripple.

Albert Einstein was a failure in school.

Even Jesus Christ came from a despised town so that people said of Him, "Can any good thing come out of Nazareth?" He was also subject to rumors of a dishonorable parentage.

When we say we are inferior, what do we actually mean? Usually we mean that in certain ways other people excel us. It is a comparison game, and how we come out depends on what trait we choose to compare. In some ways most other people excel you. In some ways you probably excel most other people.

Judging oneself either inferior or superior is also often subjective. For example, a small man may feel inferior and may be referred to by others as a shrimp or peewee. But what objective disadvantages has he? Some perhaps, but he also has advantages. Usually the compact physiology of a small man makes for better health than does the stretched-out body of someone large. In fact, tall men are almost notorious for having bad backs.

Nevertheless, let us acknowledge that some people are generally inferior to most others physically, mentally, and in talents. This brings us to the second point.

2. Our "Givens" Do Not Originate with Us and Are Neither to Our Credit nor Our Blame

The person who excels you in natural advantages has nothing whatever to justify his feeling superior. He had nothing to do with it. Is he handsome? He could have been born as ugly as Beethoven. Is he intelligent? He could have been retarded from birth. Is he physically strong? He could have been born a cripple; for that matter he could become one yet through accident or illness beyond his control.

The point is, as the Scripture says, "Who makes you different from anyone else? What do you have that you did not receive? And if you did receive it, why do you boast as though you did not?" (1 Cor. 4:7). One has no reason to be proud of his "givens" and, by the same token, one has no reason to be ashamed of them. It is God's doing, not ours.

If you understand this, "then you will not take pride in one man over against another' (v. 6). It follows then that you should not "take pride" in another over yourself; you should not feel inferior.

It is not that you should be blind to your weaknesses. That is hardly a sane self-evaluation. What you should do is decline to take as your responsibility what is God's work. Decline to take it as a personal discredit to you when others naturally excel you in some way, or even in many ways.

3. Inferior Skills Do Not Make an Inferior Person

If anyone can properly be identified as inferior, it is the person deficient in character, not in skills.

To understand this, consider the other side, the person with superior skills. Let's say a man is the world's best swimmer or chess player or test pilot. Would that make him a superior person even if he were selfish and dishonest and cruel?

He might think so, especially since the world would acclaim his accomplishments and heap praise on him. Actually, if he were of poor character, this inflating feedback from the world would only make him arrogant and thus more flawed than he was before. A graphic example of this kind is seen in Haman, whose case is examined in chapter 3.

The good news in all of this is that *you do not need to be inferior* because good character traits, which are the true marks of your quality as a person, can be developed. As the Scripture says, "Make every effort to add to your faith goodness; . . . knowledge; . . . self-control; . . . perseverance, . . . godliness, . . . brotherly kindness, . . . love" (2 Pet. 1:5-7).[1]

Assuming, then, that you do not have a poor character and no intention of changing it, we come to our fourth point.

4. God Uses "Inferior" People as Much as the Gifted

Obviously, God cannot use everyone in the same way. He is not going to use a person with no musical ability to write great symphonies or move multitudes toward God with stirring renditions in song.

Nevertheless, God can, will, and has used the weakest and most helpless of human beings wonderfully. Robert H. Schuller gives the following example:

> I think of a husband and wife who have three healthy daughters and a young son who is a mongoloid. "We love all our children equally. But we *enjoy* our son the most," the father told me. "Perhaps it is because we know the others can get along on their own. But we know that he needs us. And we all need to be needed. When I come home from work, even though I have accomplished great things in my profession of engineering, I pick up my little boy with the slanted eyes and feel his thin arms curl around my neck. I hold him tight and in that supreme moment I know that I am a very important person to him. In that divine second I have an enormous and overwhelming sense of self-worth."[2]

Surely God was using that mongoloid child.

Similarly, who has not seen or heard of God using a sick or lost child to touch the hearts of wayward parents, or even of whole communities?

The Bible abounds with examples of God using the inferior. "But God chose the foolish things of the world to shame the wise; God chose the weak things of the world to shame the strong. He chose the lowly things of this world and the despised things—and the things that are not—to nullify the things that are, so that no man may boast before him" (1 Cor. 1:27-29).

A Biblical Case Study

Every person who feels inferior ought to get an immense lift from the story of Gideon, one of the greatest of the judges of Israel.

Gideon lived in a time when the land of Israel was devastated by a foreign invader, the Midianites. Whatever the Israelites produced in crops and herds was confiscated, and the people were reduced to living like fugitives in their own land.

To belong to a nation of oppressed people does not do a whole lot for one's positive self-image in the first place, for we all have a certain group identity.[3] Gideon comes along when being an Israelite is in some ways detrimental to his self-esteem. Besides that he leads a furtive, demeaning life, trying to survive under the oppressive hand of a superior foreign power.

We see Gideon for the first time "threshing wheat in a winepress to keep it from the Midianites" (Judg. 6:11). Gideon cannot harvest any wheat in the open. He has to sneak a little of it into the winepress where he hopes he can thresh it without being detected.

"When the angel of the Lord appeared to Gideon, he said, 'The Lord is with you, mighty warrior' " (v. 12).

Do you get the irony of that greeting? "Mighty warrior"? "Timid pussycat" would better fit Gideon's actions and feelings at the time.

Then Gideon said to him, "But sir, . . . if the Lord is with us, why has all this happened to us? Where are all his wonders that our fathers told us about. . . ? But now the Lord has abandoned us" (v. 13).

Reading Gideon's responses is like reading a list of factors that damage self-esteem:

- "Why has this happened?" (I must be very bad to deserve this.)
- "Where are the wonders of our fathers?" (I don't measure up to my forebears.)
- "The Lord has abandoned us." (I'm really angry at God, but that's blasphemous. Since I can't blame Him, I have to blame me.)

The Lord then says that Gideon is to deliver Israel from the oppressor, and Gideon responds, "But Lord, . . . how can I save Israel? My clan is the weakest in Manasseh, and I am the least in my family" (v. 15).

More self-deprecating factors:

- "How can I save Israel?" (I can't do anything.)
- "My clan is the weakest." (I have no breeding.)
- "I am the least." (I get no respect.)

But the Lord said to him, "I will be with you, and you will strike down the Midianites as if they were but one man" (v. 16).

We need to notice two important things about the selection of Gideon, for they reflect how God can use us who feel inferior today as well.

First, God makes us more than we could be

otherwise. The first words spoken to Gideon were, "The Lord is with you, mighty warrior" (v. 12). As we have already observed, that description did not at all fit Gideon as he was. However, it did fit Gideon as God intended him to become.

You may be keenly aware of your inadequacies. These weaknesses and failings may be very real, not just imagined. Gideon's experience demonstrates that, in the will of God, weaknesses can actually be turned into strengths.

Instead of just bemoaning your inferiority, then, be sensitive to the voice of God calling you to become something better. People do change, you know. Perhaps certain formal training would help you. Maybe God Himself will tutor you in the school of life. However it happens, remember that if God is calling you to a work, He will also enable you to do it. "The one who calls you is faithful and he will do it" (1 Thess. 5:24).

Second, God can use us even with our limitations and inadequacies. In the midst of his protestations of unfitness, Gideon heard the Lord say, "Go in the strength you have. . . . Am I not sending you?" (Judg. 6:14).

In the glorious tradition of all great men of God, Gideon was to do exploits not because of his own might but because the Lord was using him.

The Lord can use you too. It really is true that God requires not so much our ability as our availability. He used an ordinary stick in the hand of Moses to part the waters of the Red Sea. He used an ass to rebuke the madness of Balaam the prophet. He used an obscure girl named Mary to give birth to His only begotten Son, then cradled Him in a humble cattle stall and announced the event not to heads of state but to shepherds.

Yes, and He used a once-frightened Gideon and a band of 300 men to rout a Midianite army of 135,000 soldiers.

God not only can use the inferior, but He seems to delight in doing so. As He told Gideon concerning the army of 32,000 men he had originally gathered, "You have too many men for me to deliver Midian into their hands. . . . Israel may not boast against me that her own strength has saved her" (7:2).

Barley-Loaf People

Someone says, "I like what you are teaching, but I still feel so inferior."

Yes, and God understands your doubts and fears. He knows they do not go away overnight. Gideon required signs before he could surmount his doubts. Even after twice "putting out the fleece" and seeing God act on his behalf, Gideon needed help. But the point is, he was open and responding and following God one step at a time. That is what we must do.

For Gideon, the climax came the night before the battle was to be joined. God sent his "mighty warrior" under cover of darkness to spy out the enemy camp. Even here he accommodated Gideon, saying, "If you are afraid to attack, go down to the camp with your servant Purah" (7:10). Evidently Gideon was afraid, for he did take Purah and go down.

At the edge of the enemy camp the two spies overheard a conversation between some guards. One said, "I had a dream. . . . A round loaf of barley bread came tumbling into the Midianite camp. It struck the tent with such force that the tent overturned and collapsed."

His friend answered, "This can be nothing other than the sword of Gideon. . . . God has given the Midianites and the whole camp into his hands" (7:13,14).

As you can well imagine, that was considerable encouragement to Gideon, to say the least. But don't miss the significance of the symbolism in the dream. Gideon was represented by a loaf of barley bread. Not by an armored chariot, as representing grand military might, but by a humble product of the land. Furthermore, this loaf of bread that stood for Gideon was not baked from wheat or rye or oats, as would normally be the case, but was of the cheapest and most lowly of grains—barley.

Had Gideon seen himself as the humblest member of the least family in Manasseh? Was he a nobody? OK. It was true. He wasn't from the finest of the wheat. He was coarse barley. God offered Gideon no illusions about himself to counter those marks of inferiority. He only showed that even a barley loaf, in the plan and purposes of God, could knock down and destroy the tents of Midian and bring deliverance to God's people.

God offers you no illusions either. Perhaps a sane self-evaluation will reveal you as a person not rich in natural endowments. So admit that. Accept it. But remember too that God does amazing things with barley-loaf people when they are totally available to Him.

Notes

1. For a study of the nature of these traits and how to add them to one's character, see: Stanley C. Baldwin's *How to Build Your Christian Character* (Wheaton, IL: Victor Books, 1982).

2. Robert H. Schuller, *Self-Love: The Dynamic Source of Success* (Old Tappan, NJ: Fleming H. Revell Co., 1969).

3. The group identity phenomenon shows itself curiously in professional sports. When a team gains a world championship, people from the city the team represents go wild. Even many with little interest in the game get caught up in the excitement. The players, however, are usually not "our local boys" at all. They were recruited from far and near, simply hired for the job, and in coming seasons will likely play for opposing teams. Nevertheless, just because they represent a certain city and are winning, the locals feel great pride.

The same dynamic works in reverse when one is identified with a losing or oppressed people. That's why American black leaders worked so hard to produce a "black is beautiful" consciousness in their people.

Chapter 3

The Pride Problem

"The Bible never has anything good to say for pride," the preacher thundered. "It is a word consistently used in a negative, evil sense."

I had heard it at least a hundred times before. I had preached it myself with all the conviction of "Thus saith the Lord."

Did not the brilliant archangel Lucifer fall from heaven and turn into the devil because of pride? Did not Adam and Eve fall from innocence and plunge the human race into sin because, in pride, they wanted to be like God?

Even my "sane self-evaluation" text mentions first the danger of pride: "Do not think of yourself more highly than you ought" (Rom. 12:3).

Why then, should I or any other Christian teacher seek to build people's self-esteem? Isn't self-esteem just another name for pride?

Clearly, some definitions are needed. In the New Testament, three different Greek words relate to pride. The derivations of these words are interesting and highly instructive.

Huperephanos (proud) is formed by combining *huper* (above) with *phainomai* (to appear, be manifest) and literally means "to show oneself above others." Notice the strong element of comparison. Pride, by this definition, has nothing to do with self-esteem as such but only with exalting yourself above someone else.

The second word, *tuphoo* (proud, high-minded) has its origin in *tuphos*, which means "smoke." The idea seems to be that as smoke obscures an object, so pride obscures the true nature of a person. Pride is pretense; it's putting on airs. As Romans 12:3 says, it is thinking of ourselves "more highly than we ought" to think.

A third Greek word related to pride, though not so translated, is *phusioo*, which means "to puff up or inflate." Again we have the idea of falsehood, of appearing to be bigger than we really are.

Pride, then, is exalting oneself above others or assuming a self-congratulatory stance not justified by the facts. Self-esteem, by contrast, does not depend on comparison with others. And it is based on truth not illusion.

Paul contrasts sinful pride with self-esteem when he writes, "If anyone thinks he is something when he is nothing, he deceives himself. Each one should test his own actions. Then he can take pride in himself, without comparing himself to somebody else" (Gal. 6:3,4).[1]

The Greek term translated "take pride" here is not one of the three expressions mentioned above, which are always used negatively. Here the original is *kauchema*, which means to glory or exult or boast. When the Lord here approves "glorying" in our genuinely good traits or deeds, He is encouraging self-esteem.

To clothe these various definitions in flesh and blood, let's consider a classic biblical case of a proud and arrogant man. In the entire Bible, one character seems to stand out as a supreme example of such conceit: Haman. The account is in the book of Esther, one of the best stories ever written in terms of plot, characterization, and development.

We can here consider only a part of this magnificent story, namely chapters 3-6. We will condense the story from the biblical text. As you read, try to analyze the character of Haman. What kind of person is he, and what makes him behave as he does?

"After these events, King Xerxes honored Haman son of Hammedatha, the Agagite, elevating him and giving him a seat of honor higher than that of all the other nobles. All the royal officials at the king's gate knelt down and paid honor to Haman, for the king had commanded this concerning him. But Mordecai would not kneel down or pay him honor. . . .

"When Haman saw that Mordecai would not kneel down or pay him honor, he was enraged. Yet having learned who Mordecai's people were, he scorned the idea of killing only Mordecai. Instead Haman looked for a way to destroy all Mordecai's people, the Jews, throughout the whole kingdom of Xerxes" (Esth. 3:1,2,5,6).

So Haman slandered the Jews and got the king to condemn them all to death. No one knew that Esther, the queen, was herself a Jew until after the unalterable edict went forth. Probably not knowing what to do but to trust God to work somehow, Esther got the principles together: the king, herself, and Haman for a banquet. She then scheduled a similar get-together for the next day. "Haman went out that day happy and in high spirits. But when he saw Mordecai at the king's gate and observed that he neither rose nor showed fear in his presence, he was filled with rage against Mordecai. Nevertheless, Haman restrained himself and went home.

"Calling together his friends and Zeresh, his wife, Haman boasted to them about his vast wealth, his many sons, and all the ways the king had honored him and how he had elevated him above the other nobles and officials. 'And that's not all,' Haman added. 'I'm the only person Queen Esther invited to accompany the king to the banquet she gave. And she has invited me along with the king tomorrow. But all this gives me no satisfaction as long as I see that Jew Mordecai sitting at the king's gate.'

"His wife Zeresh and all his friends said to him, 'Have a gallows built, seventy-five feet high, and ask the king in the morning to have Mordecai hanged on it. Then go with the king to the dinner and be happy.' This suggestion delighted Haman, and he had the gallows built.

"That night the king could not sleep; so he ordered the book of the chronicles, the record of his reign, to be brought in and read to him" (5:9—6:1).

Did the king think if anything would put him to sleep, it would be the history books? We don't know, but here we see clearly the hand of God, who is not once mentioned in the entire book. It is on this particular night before Haman is to ask Mordecai's execution that the king can't sleep, and the particular part of the history the king reads has to do with Mordecai once saving the kingdom by reporting a conspiracy.

" 'What honor and recognition has Mordecai received for this?' the king asked.

" 'Nothing has been done for him,' his attendants answered.

"The king said, 'Who is in the court?' Now Haman had just entered the outer court of the palace to speak to the king about hanging Mordecai on the gallows he had erected for him.

"His attendants answered, 'Haman is standing in the court.'

" 'Bring him in,' the king ordered.

"When Haman entered, the king asked him, 'What should be done for the man the king delights to honor?'

"Now Haman thought to himself, 'Who is there that the king would rather honor than me?' " (6:3-6)

Thinking it was for him, Haman cooked up the best rewards he could think of: to wear the king's robe and crown while being paraded through the city on the king's horse, escorted by one of the king's noblest princes and proclaimed to everyone as "the man the king delights to honor" (v. 9).

Imagine the shock, the crestfallen face, the leaden heart with which Haman heard the king's next words:

" 'Go at once,' the king commanded Haman. 'Get the robe and the horse and do just as you have suggested for Mordecai the Jew, who sits at the king's gate. Do not neglect anything you have recommended' " (v. 10).

The story continues with other delightful twists and turns. We will not pursue it further, however, but will seek to analyze the character of

Haman. What can we observe about him from the record?

The most revealing insight into Haman's character comes from his own mouth. "I'm the only person Queen Esther invited to accompany the king to the banquet she gave" (5:12). There you have it, the dead giveaway. Haman's self-image hinges on comparing himself with others. Would it matter if someone else had attended the banquet too? Can't another receive equal recognition without it detracting from him?

Another could, if Haman's self-esteem were properly based on himself alone. But not if he is proud, not if he must show himself above others because his excellence is only so much smoke, so much puff.

Another key to Haman's character is his intense concern over what people think of him. Clearly, it is not self-interest that drives Haman so much as self-glorification. He already has everything a person might be expected to want, the highest position in the kingdom. Yet he says, "All this gives me no satisfaction as long as I see that Jew Mordecai sitting at the king's gate" (5:13).

We see his insatiable hunger for glorification again when he tells the king what honors should be heaped on his head.

This adulation compulsion reveals that Haman based his self-evaluation on the feedback he got from his world. Since that world praised him lavishly, he had an exaggerated opinion of himself. But when one man refused to defer to him, the entire structure on which his self-esteem rested was threatened. He determined to destroy a whole race of people in order to preserve his fragile self-esteem.

The interesting thing is that Haman was probably by nature an able and likable person. How else could he have achieved the striking success that was his? After all, he was not born to prominence; he rose to it. But because he based his self-esteem on the world's feedback, a sane self-evaluation was impossible for Haman. What a tragedy!

The tragedy was by no means Haman's alone however. He might have been of great service to God and the people with his energy, ingenuity, and power. Instead the man became vicious, destructive, virtually an insane killer.

While you and I may never reach the same level of prominence Haman did, the principles observable in his life operate in us as well.

Who suffers if you or I lack a sane self-evaluation?

We do, but so does everyone else whose life we touch. We may become hateful and violent like Haman. Or the mischief may be much more subtle. Our disorder may betray itself only by a cutting remark about another person, a remark that slips out without our realizing why.

Our pride can also destroy Christian fellowship and damage the community of believers by producing in us a spirit of aloofness, as it did in Jennifer, whom you will meet in the next chapter. There too we'll seek insight into how and why a low self-esteem often coexists with pride. And we'll see how one person escaped such a double bind.

Note

1. Here the Bible does use pride in a good sense, contrary to the preacher quoted earlier. He was correct, however, that "pride" is never used favorably in the King James version.

Chapter 4

Living in a Hall of Mirrors

Ah, good old Jantzen Beach! It's not what it used to be. What a glorious place it was when I was young! The roller coaster—so terrifying I rode it only once. The swimming pools—one with a high diving board I also dove from only once. I hurt my neck a little and from then on it was strictly feet first off the high board for me.

There were the bumper cars—what sheer pleasure, and the fun house and dozens of other attractions. But it's all gone now. Today the site bordering the Columbia River where one enters Oregon from Vancouver, Washington is occupied by a luxurious conference center/lodge and various other business enterprises. They are nice. And the amusement park was getting run down, I suppose. Still, it seems kind of a shame . . .

I remember the hall of mirrors. How we laughed at the way those mirrors made us look. One made me short and fat, the next tall and thin. One gave me a tall thin face and a short fat body, while another made me look like the crooked man who walked a crooked mile.

The hall of mirrors was a fun place to visit. One wouldn't want to live there, though. How would a person ever know what he really looked like?

But suppose for a moment that one lived in a house with only the short fat type mirror. How could he escape seeing himself as short and fat? In time he would grow so accustomed to that image that even if he did happen to gaze upon a true reflection he would discount it as the unrepresentative one.

Some people live with similar distortions psychologically. Their milieu regularly reflects an image of them that is one-sided and false. All of us, even if we are not in that situation, either live in a hall of mirrors or at least pass through one continually for our world reflects all kinds of distorted images of us.

No wonder people get confused about their identities. They get conflicting information all the time.

As I recall, the hall of mirrors at Jantzen Beach had one unique mirror which a person came to last. It gave a true and undistorted reflection of the person standing before it. It kind of restored one's sanity—reminded him what he actually looked like and reassured him that all the grotesque distortions were that.

We have such a mirror for our personalities. The Bible says: "Do not merely listen to the word, and so deceive yourselves. Do what it says. Anyone who listens to the word but does not do what it says is like a man who looks at his face in a mirror and, after looking at himself, goes away and immediately forgets what he looks like" (Jas. 1:22-24).

The Word of God reflects us as we truly are. But we must look at this true reflection enough to correct the confusion that comes from passing through the hall of mirrors. We must look often enough and long enough so that we do not forget what we look like.

If we look into God's Word sufficiently we will know, for example, that the world's praise for some conspicuous achievement does not mean we are Superior People, unflawed. We will also know that the world's criticism, though it comes in a hundred forms or more, does not mean we are Inferior People, unworthy.

Without God's mirror, though, we are likely to hold both aforementioned illusions at the same time, even though that doesn't make sense. That is, a person can be both proud and self-despising at the same time. In fact, this is not only possible but common.

Often the very lack of self-esteem causes us to grasp for something to compensate for that lack. We desperately want to feel good about ourselves, to be praiseworthy. So, fighting against whatever reflects upon us adversely, we become oversensitive, thin-skinned, defensive. And latching on to whatever makes us look good, we become proud, vainglorious, and critical of others.

Jennifer was caught in this double bind of pride and low self-esteem existing in the same person at the same time. By nature she is outgoing. Her thoughts and feelings surface easily. However, Jennifer found herself in a relationship in which her self-expression was often put down.

Actually, in the early stages of this relationship with her husband, Jennifer *was* wrong most of the time. She was a young, naive, hippy-type girl barely out of her teens. She didn't know the Lord and had little training in the Scriptures.

Ben was a strong Christian and an active outdoor evangelist. He met Jennifer on the street, led her to the Lord, and eventually married her. He became not only her leader/teacher but her leader/husband.

As the years passed, however, and Jennifer grew to maturity as a Christian, the old way of relating that was established between them continued. Whatever she said or did that disagreed with Ben's views, he judged, condemned, or criticized. Jennifer felt enormous pressure to conform to whatever Ben wanted her to be, to think, to do.

Deferring to Ben as she did, Jennifer also developed a deferential attitude toward others whom she saw as her superiors. She assumed they too expected her to conform to their ideas of what she should do and be. So she played roles. Whatever the Superior People wanted her to do and be, she attempted. But trying to be what she thought each person wanted led to great confusion. Which role was really Jennifer?

As poor as her self-esteem problem was, however, Jennifer also had a pride problem. Ben had taught her the classical legalistic Christianity that governed his life: a list of narrowly prescribed dos and don'ts. Jennifer kept all the rules on the list quite well and that became her badge of merit.

In her pride, Jennifer judged other people by whether or not they obeyed her list of rules. Most fell far short of her requirements. Jennifer could have no fellowship with such people because they were compromisers, unfaithful Christians. Since they obviously didn't mean business about living for Jesus, she couldn't waste much time on them.

Meanwhile, those who were spiritual in Jennifer's eyes, she almost revered. They were on a pedestal, and all she could do was try to be what they would approve. Consequently, Jennifer had no true fellowship with them either. She was virtually alone emotionally.

This went on for about nine years. A change began when the proud, rule-keeping Jennifer opened her heart just a wee bit to wonder if there might actually be some hidden sins in her own life that she didn't even know about. The Lord began to speak to her about the sins of the heart: bitterness, anger, jealousy, envy. And pride. When God showed her how proud she had been in her attitude toward Christians who were "beneath her," Jennifer was devastated. She literally cried and repented for a week.

When Jennifer repented of her pride, she no longer had that substitute for wholesome self-esteem. This enabled her, over the next two years, to see how much she lacked it.

The Lord had shown Jennifer how invalid, how *wrong*, it was for her to judge others. She had realized that the failings she thought she saw in them were not necessarily worse than failings she did not see in herself.

Slowly she began to realize that for anyone to have a judgmental, critical attitude toward her was just as wrong as for her to have such an attitude. Other Christians did not have to be what she thought they should be; they were accountable to God, not to her. By the same token, she didn't have to be what someone else, even Ben, thought she should be. She was accountable to God.

What a glorious freedom this brought!

It meant she didn't have to roleplay any more. She didn't have to try to be what others thought she should be. She only had to be who she was, in a humble walk with her heavenly Father.

Jennifer had escaped from the hall of mirrors.

But it only happened when she let the Holy Spirit show her a reflection of the truth, a truth she didn't really want to see at first, but a truth that has set her free.

Chapter 5

An Appeal to Diotrephes

An earnest letter from the author to a first-century brother in error.

How I long to reach out to you, dear brother!

Ordinarily, in circumstances such as these I wouldn't intrude. Even now, if it were simply a matter of personality clash between you and John, I'd keep silent. But it's for love of our dear Lord Jesus that I speak, for I'm sure He must be deeply grieved.

John says he corresponded with your church, anticipating a visit there, but that you oppose him, speak against him and others not of your party, and even impose sanctions against those in your fellowship who want to receive these brothers.

This you do, he says, because you love "to be first" (3 John 9).

Dear brother, I suppose there is in all of us some desire to be first. But I can't help thinking of what it must do to our Lord Jesus to see this vying for preeminence within His church. He was so vehement against that kind of thing as it manifested itself in the old system.

Surely you remember how incensed our Lord was over the way the Pharisees jockeyed for position. Did He not pronounce seven "woes" on them in one day? And why? Partly at least because "they love the place of honor at banquets and the most important seats in the synagogues; they love to be greeted in the marketplaces and to have men call them 'Rabbi.' "

Remember what He said then, after castigating the Pharisees? "You are not to be called 'Rabbi,' for you have only one Master and you are all brothers" (Matt. 23:6,8).

Now to see within His own church the very evil for which He denounced the Pharisees—well, how must it make Him feel?

What is the source of this compulsion to occupy first place? Some might say it is pride, and I suppose they are right since it is a seeking after comparative advantage, after a place of eminence over others. Still I cannot but believe that a lack of self-esteem underlies it all; for when one really feels good about himself deep down, he has no need to grasp for importance by dominating his brothers.

I do not write this to take anything away from you, dear Diotrephes, for that, as I see it, is the problem already. You are operating from a deficit. I would give to you, if I could, the inner adequacy, the profound sense of worth, the self-esteem that would make you secure in yourself without dominating others.

Our beloved brother Paul has written "to everyone of you," and I'm sure that means you, Diotrephes, as well as me: "Do not think of yourself more highly than you ought, but rather think of yourself with sober judgment" (Rom. 12:3). He told us not to be conformed to the pattern of this world. Not to get our self-image from the world's feedback. Not to scramble like worldly people for some edge over others. But to be transformed by a renewed mind from God.

I beg of you to consider a few principles on which such a renewed mind may be based. Though the words may sound familiar, please ponder the implications with me so that our minds may be transformed by these truths. We will be safeguarded then against the distortions both of pride and self-reproach that mar so many.

First, dear Diotrephes, you and I are . . .

Made in God's Image (see Gen. 1:27)

Our unbelieving friends have missed this truth completely. They live without ultimate meaning or purpose or dignity because they see themselves only as the chance products of mindless evolution. They still grope for some reason for being, of course, because they need it. But they have no logical basis either for wanting self-esteem or for obtaining it.

You and I, dear brother, are not so forlorn. Yet, as I say, the far-reaching implications of the truth we so familiarly embrace often seem to escape us—even as they escaped Eve. For if she were made in the image of God, why was she subject to the tempter's suggestion that by eating the forbidden fruit she could become "like God" (Gen. 3:5)?

I know there was more to the temptation than that. Yet, Eve must have been somehow unaware of her likeness to God or she'd not have sought to obtain what was already hers.

And you, O Diotrephes, if you realized your own Godlikeness would have no need for this playing God with the lives of others. Indeed, like the blessed Son of God, you could put aside even your legitimate privileges, not counting them something to be grasped, and could humble yourself to servanthood.

You see, Jesus was still the express image of God no matter how much He humbled Himself, and He knew it. You too can become secure enough in your image-of-God identity that you will not need to bolster your sense of worth by dominating others.

The psalmist wrote concerning man: "You made him a little lower than God and crowned him with glory and honor" (Ps. 8:5, see footnote in *NIV*). Surely this God-assigned place should be enough for any mortal man, don't you think? I'm sure you would at once accept that you are at best "a little lower than God." But if so, remember, your brothers and sisters are only a little lower than God as well. If you exalt yourself above them, you intrude into the Lord's domain. I don't think you want to do that. It was that kind of presumption that led to the fall of Lucifer.

You and I, Diotrephes, not only are made in the image of God but also are . . .

Significant to the Life of God

"Are not five sparrows sold for two pennies? Yet not one of them is forgotten by God. Indeed, the very hairs of your head are all numbered. Don't be afraid; you are worth more than many sparrows" (Luke 12:6,7).

"Don't be afraid," Jesus says.

Afraid?

Diotrephes, you of all people project self-assurance. You are competent, strong, authoritative, a leader. But could it be the Lord Jesus sees something else in you? Something hidden from others and perhaps even from yourself? Could it be that somewhere under all that strength you display, there lives a frightened man? A man who can feel secure only when he is in complete control?

"You are worth more than many sparrows," Jesus says. Is it possible that underneath your self-assured manner the Lord sees someone doubtful of his own worth?

You know, Diotrephes, we all need to sense that we are of value. Even my small grandchildren are forever coming to me for recognition. "Look, Grandpa, see what I made." Currently the youngest is so proud of her latest accomplishment that she spontaneously thanks God every night in her prayers for her potty-chair.

We all reach for significance, but not always in constructive ways. Some become servile, sycophantic, like Jennifer was. Some knock themselves out to reach impressive heights. Some lash out at others, and a few have even killed famous people. And some, O Diotrephes, have chosen the path of domination, grabbing for stature by controlling those around them.

The deep inner deficit in our feeling of significance that gives rise to these destructive life-styles is an evidence of world conformity. The renewed mind, by contrast, thinks as Jesus said we should. "Don't be afraid," He said. We can relax, then, secure in our standing with Him.

"You are worth more than many sparrows," He

said. We need not feel driven, then, to establish our value for He has already conferred worth upon us.

Now we need only make ourselves available to Him who says: "I know the plans that I have for you, . . . plans to prosper you and not to harm you, plans to give you hope and a future" (Jer. 29:11).

Think of it. God has plans for you. It's almost as if you received a personal message:

> Dear Diotrephes:
> Relax. You matter to me.
> I have good plans for you.
> And I never forget you for a moment.
> Signed: *God*

Have I overstated the facts?

David didn't think so. He wrote: "How precious it is, Lord, to realize that you are thinking about me constantly! I can't even count how many times a day your thoughts turn towards me. And when I waken in the morning, you are still thinking of me!" (Ps. 139:17,18, *TLB*).

A Personal Word

I must draw this letter to a close for I have already imposed upon your patience. Permit me only this further word of witness.

I, too, have endured the pain of personal insecurity. And I, too, have seen that insecurity mar my fellowship with others, though not in just the same way you are experiencing. Instead of trying to dominate people, I tended to stand off from them, to keep my distance. I was defensive, withdrawn. I figured that what others did not know about my business couldn't hurt me.

This attitude led to much misunderstanding and unnecessary suffering. One particular experience symbolized my life then. It happened one winter during the austere early days of my Bible training. I was living with my little family in extremely humble quarters in a small town far from my ancestral home. We were very poor.

Since I didn't feel I could possibly afford garbage service, whenever the wastes accumulated to the point where something had to be done, I tried to bury them out in the yard. The ground was frozen rock-hard, however, so I couldn't bury anything very deep.

I was out there one day, scratching at the frozen earth and realizing I wasn't digging deep enough, when a fellow student who was a local resident passed by. He called a friendly greeting from the road and would have engaged me in conversation but I was short with him. I didn't want him to know what I was doing.

As a result, I not only turned away a brother who wanted to be a friend but I also prevented myself from learning what he surely would have told me at once—that in their town municipal garbage service was provided without charge to all residents.

I'm sorry to say, Diotrephes, that experience taught me nothing. It was only as the Lord dealt with the underlying problem—my insecurity and low self-esteem—that I began to overcome my defensiveness and withdrawal.

To deal with that underlying self-image problem, the Lord used the very principles I have here shared with you. Someone helped me to see what it means to be made in the image of God and what it means to be the object of God's loving care.

Other passages of Scripture spoke to me as well. I read in Ephesians the prayer of Paul that my eyes might be opened to see that God considered me His rich and "glorious inheritance" (Eph. 1:18). That was such a revelation to me that I began preaching it everywhere and later wrote a book on Ephesians to share that good news.[1]

The familiar benediction from Jude that I had pronounced over so many congregations also took on rich, new meaning. "To him who is able to keep you from falling and to present you before his glorious presence without fault and with great joy" it says (v. 24).

What a thrill it was to realize that Jesus is not going to sneak me in some back door of heaven. He is going to *present* me formally to the Father. And when He does it will not be with shame or with any hint of reluctance on His part but with *great joy*.

With that kind of acceptance awaiting me in heaven—and mine already with Jesus—I was enabled to accept myself much more than I ever could before. And to feel secure.

Oh, receive these truths, dear Diotrephes, and cast off the old ways of thinking. Insecurity and self-reproach, with all their attendant ills, have no place in your life as a believer. The good news is that you do not need to depend on your own inadequate efforts to dispose of this refuse. Heaven's garbage service is free.

Note

1. Stanley C. Baldwin, *What Makes You So Special?* (Grand Rapids: Baker Book House, 1977).

PART II
How to Handle Your Handle

Chapter 6

What's in Your Name?

The woman was past 40 years of age. Yet as she described an experience of her youth, her voice trembled with emotion. The wound had been so deep, the pain so great that even now she had difficulty dealing with the memory.

"I was somewhat overweight as a girl," she told me, "and my father had this terrible nickname for me. He called me Fats. How I hated it! He would go to the front door and call me in from play, 'Fats, come home.'

"I can still see myself sneaking in through the backyard lest anyone see me responding to that awful name."

We've said earlier, you will remember, that our self-concept is greatly influenced by the feedback we get from others. One powerful example of this has to do with our names.

Think of it. Your name, the label that identifies you as a person, was arbitrarily assigned you by others. Usually, in Western culture, our names are selected by our parents with little or no consideration of any meaning they may have. Not so with nicknames. They are often pinned on us because of their meaning. Thus a derogatory nickname becomes a direct assault on our self-image.

Fats is one example. Slim, Tiny, Slats, Shorty, and Red may be others. Or to cite well-known people, how would you like to be called Ugly Ike, as President Eisenhower was early in life? Or Tricky Dick, as President Nixon was long before Watergate?

I grew up with a nickname problem myself, so I understand a little what Fats and others have endured. My family called me Babe. I didn't mind so much when I was small and only family was around. But when I grew into my teens and had friends over, it became painful.

"What did they call you?" one of them asked after a visit to our home. "Babe?" And then he snickered.

It was a good thing he never heard my mother's pet name for me: Lambkin. I never would have lived that down. Maybe my dad sensed that such nicknames would be a source of embarrassment to me sooner or later. In any case, he had his own compensating nickname for me and I loved the sound of it. He called me Tuffy. But my dad died when I was 10, and "Tuffy" died with him.

Names Do Make a Difference

According to the nineteenth-century poet-essayist James Russell Lowell, "there is more force in names than most men dream." Recent studies have tended to support that idea, both in the case of nicknames and formal names.

Dr. Robert C. Nicolay and his colleagues at Chicago's Loyola University studied 10,000 criminal offenders over a period of five years. Their conclusion was, in Nicolay's own words, "There is without a doubt a significantly higher frequency of psychosis leading to criminal behavior in the peculiar name group."

It has been observed by others that the outstanding leaders of American society—college presidents, topflight business executives, the wealthy elite—also have a disproportionate number of odd names. Thus a distinctive name often corresponds with a distinctive career, though that career may be for the better or the worse.

Studies also indicate that certain common names generally contribute to, while others hinder, an individual's chances of—

- achieving an equitable grade in scholastic work
- getting hired for a responsible position
- winning an election to public office.

People are prejudiced about names, and if they don't like yours it can hurt your chances.

The entertainment industry seems especially sensitive to the potential impact of one's name on one's career. Thus, the entertainer who works under his or her original name is the exception rather than the rule.

And what about Ann Landers and Abigail Van Buren? Would these twin sisters have achieved their great success as advice columnists if readers had been told to write Esther (Eppie) Friedman Lederer or Pauline (Popo) Friedman Phillips?

Usually, however, even the person who heartily dislikes his or her name is hesitant about the idea of changing it. One of the few books that deals with the psychological effect of names gives the following example.

> One who stuck it out was *Future Shock* author Alvin Toffler. "I hate Alvin," he states flatly. "I have always hated it. Alvin was a sissy name, and I was constantly getting into fistfights over it—even in high school. Thank God, I grew up in the 1940s and not the 1950s. I might have had to live down 'Alvin the Chipmunk' on top of all the rest."[1]

The same book tells of a man who changed both his public image and his self-image by changing his name. Carlton Fredericks is a nutritionist and consumer advocate.

> "Your mother must have had a hunch you'd be a celebrity," marveled one interviewer. "Carlton Fredericks is the perfect name for someone in public life." Actually, Fredericks started out as Harold Casper Fredericks Caplan, and suffered the misfortune of being known simply as Casper by his doting mother. By the time he was nine, Fredericks recalls, "I knew that Casper was something I just couldn't handle. I was squabbling over my name every week. It got so I cringed whenever a teacher called on me in class. So at my insistence, my mother marched down to City Hall and we had my name legally changed to Carlton Fredericks."
>
> Why Carlton? "The Carltons were cousins, and I always thought that it had such a nice—no, an important—sound. It made a definite change as far as my self-esteem was concerned, and in turn I

found that the other kids were finally treating me with some respect."[2]

To Change or Not to Change

As a result of my studies in preparing this chapter, I'm thinking of changing my name. If the cover of this book lists the author as S. Conrad Baldwin, you'll know I did it. (Conrad is my middle name, a fact that was once a closely guarded secret.) If I'm still going by Stanley C. Baldwin, I either decided against the change or couldn't make up my mind.

What do you think? Would a book by S. Conrad Baldwin carry a bit more weight with you than one by Stanley C. Baldwin? How about Stan Baldwin?

In the United States, changing one's name is usually a simple matter. If you are not changing with some criminal intent, no legal process is required. You can simply adopt a new name, though obviously some confusion and negative consequences may result.

On the other hand, one young man was refused a legal name change in Minnesota a few years ago. He wanted his new name to be "1069." The judge rebuked him for "an offense to human dignity" and said a number for a name was "inherently totalitarian."

To which I can almost hear a certain woman reply, "An offense to human dignity? What do you think Fats is?"

And to which, in turn, most of us would probably say, "Yes, that too should have been against the law."

A New Name from God

Beyond having proper names and good or bad

nicknames, we also receive from the world a name relating to our reputation. It is to this that Scripture refers when it says, "A good name is more desirable than great riches" (Prov. 22:1).

A girl can get a bad name, deservedly or otherwise, and decent guys will shun her while those "looking for some action" will take her out for that reason alone.

A person can get a bad name as a credit risk and be disqualified from buying a home or other commodity. A bad name in one's vocation can make it difficult to find work, can even finish one's career. A bad name as a neighbor can mean virtual ostracism in the community.

In each and every case we've mentioned, the bad name affects more than one's public image; it assaults the self-image as well.

We have said that though most of us get our self-concept from the world, such a source is unreliable. A correct self-concept must come from God. The same thing may be said about our name, which is so closely linked to our self-concept.

Let's examine the Scriptures to learn what God does about people's names. You will be encouraged to see how He gives people good names to replace bad or mediocre ones. Yes, God loves to confer on His people wonderful names that stretch them and inspire them and lead them to become more than they were before. To become more than anybody, except God, thought they ever could be.

Take Abraham. His name was originally Abram, meaning "High Father." That was not a bad name to begin with; fathers were much honored in the patriarchal society of that day.

The trouble was that Abram had great difficulty in living up to his name. His struggle to have a child forms the backdrop for the epic story unfolded in Genesis 12—21, a story spanning some 25 years of Abram's life. It is a story of repeated frustration as childless Abram continually fell short of the meaning of his name.

At last, when Abram was 86 years old, Ishmael was born to him and Hagar, his wife's servant. So Abram did become a father, but there was nothing particularly noble or high about it, and "High Father" still seemed quite beyond him.

It was at this point, when Abram hadn't fully attained the implications of his original name, that God changed his name to Abraham, meaning "Father of a Multitude." God said he would become such a father not through Ishmael but through a son yet to be born to Sarah, his wife. This possibility seemed so remote to Abraham that he "fell facedown" and "laughed" (Gen. 17:17).

That's the way God's new names are. He sees more in us than our parents do. He sees more in us than the people around us do. He sees more in us than we do. So much more that when we hear His name for us, we too may be tempted to laugh.

But Abraham quit laughing when he realized it was up to him to choose whether or not he was going to believe this message. The most critical choice of Abraham's long and eventful life faced him at that moment, for actually his very soul's salvation depended on it.

What does the Bible say about Abraham's choice?

First, he openly faced the facts of his case. Abraham didn't just say, "OK, God, swell, I believe that I will be Father of a Multitude through Sarah." An easy statement such as that, devoid of any wrestling with the implications and difficulties, would also have been devoid of reality. You see, faith is not superficial. It's facing the issues honestly and still choosing to believe deeply.

Concerning Abraham, we read, "He faced the fact that his own body was as good as dead—since he was about a hundred years old—and that Sarah's womb was also dead" (Rom. 4:19). These were the facts that made Abraham laugh when he first heard his new name.

However, a new fact now entered the picture. God had said, "Your name will be Abraham, for *I have made you* a father of many nations" (Gen. 17:5, italics added).

Abraham's choice, then, after facing the facts, was either to believe what God said or to believe what he and everyone else "knew," that he and Sarah were unable to have children, period.

Your choice is similar. You will believe what you and others "always knew" about your being an inferior person, or you will believe something better about yourself because God says it.

The reason Abraham and you can believe the something better is not only that God says it. The reason is that the God who says it is also the Creator, and He can make it come to pass, regardless of your apparent natural potential. We are not talking here about simple positive thinking. All the positive thinking in the world could not make a 100-year-old man sexually potent and his sterile and aged wife fertile. But God could.

That is what Abraham believed. He believed in a God who "calls things that are not as though they were" (Rom. 4:17). That faith, we read, was "credited to him as righteousness" (v. 22). In other words, his soul's salvation depended on it, as we indicated a bit earlier.

Ultimately, in full implementation of the promise, Abraham did become father of a multitude. Furthermore, and here's the point we must not miss, although the promise took a long time to materialize fully, Abraham got most of its benefits then and there, for he saw himself in a completely different light. Instead of the barely-a-father-by-questionable-means image of himself that had controlled him, he now saw himself as what God said he would become: Abraham, father of many nations.

Do I have to say that Abraham lived as a happier and better man with his new self-image? Why, even his wife's name was changed at that time, and Sarai (Contentious) became Sarah (Princess). The Father of a Multitude and his Princess may have lived in the same old tent for a while after that, but I tell you it was a noble dwelling to them for they were noble people.

A New Name for the Successful Person

What God did for Abraham in replacing an old deficient self-concept with a new and glorious name, He also did for others who chose to believe Him.

Jacob was a pretty rotten guy, full of cute little tricks for taking advantage of people. Usually they worked, if getting what you want and not caring how you get it can be called working.

But how does a guy like that feel about himself? Oh, he may justify what he does. He may cover up. But deep inside, he can't like himself very much, can he?

Then, too, a person's devious behavior has a way of catching up with him eventually. After all, people don't appreciate shabby treatment. Some have even been known to retaliate. Perhaps the worst part is that a Jacob never knows for sure what the people he has misused may be thinking. Thus, even after 20 years' absence from home, Jacob feared that his brother Esau, whom he had cheated, might still be laying for him, looking to get even.

With all this garbage from his past life bugging him, Jacob had a memorable encounter one night with the Lord. There he received a new name, *Israel*. Jacob's new name meant "God's fighter," or "One who has power with God."

The point of all this is that even "successful" people have needs. You may not be a helpless, self-pitying clod. In fact, you may despise such weak people and see yourself as a resourceful, make-things-happen person who can take care of yourself. You are a fighter, a person of power. But are you God's fighter? Do you have any power with God?

If you are nowhere with God, your very strengths may lead you into disaster. Like Jacob, you may have habits and personality traits that make you successful but deep down also make you feel rotten about yourself. What about the people you associated with along the way? How did you treat them? How about your loved ones? What do they think of your priorities? How about your enemies? What could they say truthfully to your shame?

It's not that God necessarily wants to take the fight out of you. He may just want to change your name from "Dirty Fighter" to "God's Fighter." In any case, the point is that God has a name for you, and it's a good one. You need to plug it into your mental computer in place of all the bad names you've picked up elsewhere along the way. In the next chapter, we'll see just how to do that.

Notes

1. Chris Anderson, *The Name Game* (New York: BJ Publishing Group, 1979), p. 19.
2. Ibid., p. 20.

Chapter 7

A Name to Grow Into

Usually, though not always, we get our bad names for a reason. The girl mentioned in the previous chapter whose father called her Fats was fat. Nevertheless, the trouble with calling her Fats was twofold. First, it ignored everything else about her and focused on one undesirable trait as if that were the entire person. Second, it tended to perpetuate the negative trait by causing the person to think of herself in those terms.

If God had operated the way Fats's father did, He would never have called Abram Abraham or Jacob Israel. If Jesus had operated as Fats's father did, He never would have given Simon the new name Peter.

Simon was a disciple of Jesus but he was a shifting-sand type of person. Unreliable. His most notorious failure came when he three times denied he even knew Jesus. This happened only hours after he had promised Jesus he would die with Him if necessary, rather than ever to deny Him.

Yet when Jesus first met Simon, three years earlier, He changed his name to Peter, which means Rock. It took a long time for Peter to become a rock, but he'd never have been one if Jesus hadn't named him that.

You see, God's way is not to give us a good name *after* we've earned it. That's how we get our bad names. We reveal some flaw and the world saddles us with a corresponding negative identity. God's way is to give us a good, new name not typical of what we now are but of what He wants us to become, a *name to grow into.*

Guess what. It works!

See Peter standing rock-like before the enemies of the gospel, men who have power to put him to death, even as they have crucified his Lord. Hear his voice ring out: "God has made this Jesus, whom you crucified, both Lord and Christ." And again, "You killed the author of life, but God raised him from the dead" (Acts 2:36; 3:15). Then ask yourself whether it makes any difference what name a person bears. Ask if it matters whether you receive God's new name for you or not.

What is God's new name for you? The Bible calls those who have received Jesus Christ by several very special and very meaningful names. For example, "How great is the love the Father has lavished on us, that we should be called . . . "

What?

Do you know?

". . . that we should be called *children of God*" (1 John 3:1, italics added).

Child of God

The practice of naming a person by his parentage is common in many cultures. For example, in Scandinavian countries names often end with "son" (Johnson, Olson, Nelson). In Ireland a person may be said to come of Shea, of Malley, or of Rourke, contracted to O'Shea, O'Malley, or O'Rourke. In the Bible, the prefix Ben or Bar was attached to names, as in Simon Barjona, meaning son of Jonah (see Matt. 16:17).

Now, when by virtue of receiving Christ, you are called a son of God or a child of God, this is not a name just casually tossed your way. It is thoughtfully conferred upon you by God Himself and represents a drastic change from the names you were previously called: child of the devil, child of wrath, and child of hell.

No wonder John exclaims that being called a child of God is an evidence of lavish love on God's part.

Remember we said earlier that our self-concept, to be correct, must not be conditioned on the world's judgments. What the world calls us must not be allowed to determine how we see ourselves. This works both ways. The world may call you a wonderful person, but without Christ you are a miserable sinner in God's sight. Or the world may dismiss you as beneath notice. But as a Christian you are nothing less than a child of God Himself.

What this new name can do for the person who comes to grips with the reality of it is exemplified by the experience of Jim Mallory. Dr. Mallory was a physician and an active church member before he came to know Christ as personal Saviour. As a successful and respected man in the community, he wouldn't be expected to have any self-image problems, right? Wrong. Like everyone else, he was susceptible to a distorted self-evaluation from his world.

Dr. Mallory writes:

> The most immediate thing Christ did for me after my conversion was to give me a new identity. I was driving down Colonial Boulevard in Orlando shortly after my conversion, thinking about what had happened in my life, and it suddenly hit me that I *had eternal life now*. It was not something off in the future. I remember smiling, as I drove along, at the realization that I am a joint heir with Christ, a child of God, that I am part of God's family, that God has plans for me, and as I make myself available to Him, really exciting things are in store for me.
>
> This new identity was very meaningful for me, because as a youngster I was always trying to compensate for being scrawny and red headed. And now I was a son of God![1]

You see, inside the respected doctor there lived for many years a scrawny red-headed kid. Only when he received God's new name for him was Jim Mallory freed from the liabilities of his childhood.

What about you?

What unworthy self-concept are you carrying around inside? Replace it with the divinely bestowed name: Child of God.

Saint

Sinner! Sinner! Sinner! Many of us have sinned so much and been confronted with it so often that we wear that name as our badge. It's one of those bad names we talked about earlier, one that we got because we deserved it. Now we are stuck with it, even though, if we are Christians, God has given us a different name. He calls us not sinner but *saint.*

Don't laugh. Or if you do, go back and read the previous chapter again. Remember, Abraham at first thought his new name was fall-on-your-face funny. It wasn't.

Neither is yours. In fact, *saint* is the most common name in the New Testament for those who have trusted in Christ. It sounds strange to many contemporary ears because the idea persists that a saint is some rare, super-holy Christian.

However, the apostle Paul called all the Christians "saints" in his letters to the various churches of his time. *Saint* means "holy." Yet, even the Corinthians, who were perhaps the least holy in practice, were called saints repeatedly. How come?

The answer is twofold. First of all, as these very Christians were told, "God made him who had no sin to be sin for us, so that in him we might become the righteousness of God" (2 Cor. 5:21). That is, because Christ's holiness was put to their account when they received Him, they were holy in God's sight.

The second reason God called them saints is that He intended them to become holy in practice. Saint was a name they were to grow into. Sinner was a name they were to cast off as no longer descriptive of them.

Thus Paul mentions various sinner types—idolaters, thieves, sex perverts, slanderers—and then says, "And that is what some of you were. But you were washed, you were sanctified, you were justified in the name of the Lord Jesus Christ and by the Spirit of our God" (1 Cor. 6:11). Note that the passage says sinner is what you *were*, not what you are. In fact, Scripture teaches that our old sinful man is dead, crucified with Christ, and we are to count ourselves "dead to sin but alive to God in Christ Jesus" (Rom. 6:11).

This teaches nothing less than that we are to exchange our old self-image for a new one: sinner for saint. To go through life adding a propositional put-down from the Bible—you are a sinner—to all the other put-downs we must cope with is to let Satan use God's truth to his own ends. God wants us to acknowledge our sinfulness, yes, and then move on into the new life of the redeemed.

We will have more to say on this great theme in chapter 10. For now, let us simply observe that many Christians, tragically, have only worsened an already poor self-image by a distorted application of Christian truth. They have bought the proposition that they are worthless sinners and have gotten stuck there.

An experience I had back in Bible institute illustrates the point. The teacher had asked us to write on the subject, "What did Jesus see of value in man?" He explained that he did not want us to say that there was nothing of value in man for Jesus to see.

When the papers came in, what do you suppose they said? Many (including mine, I fear) said that man is a totally depraved sinner with nothing in him that could possibly be of any value to God. We supported our staunch orthodoxy with Scripture: "There is no one righteous, not even one. . . . All have turned away, they have together become worthless" (Rom. 3:10,12). "For all have sinned and fall short of the glory of God" (v. 23).

We really knew that man is a sinner. And that's good. But we did not understand the full implications of the fact that, so far as God is concerned, man is a sinner worth saving.

Notice, we are saying that even the natural man has worth, though he is the enemy of God. If God loved us while we were His enemies, and saw us as worth saving even at the cost of the Cross, what does He think of us now that we are His friends? (see Rom. 5:6-11).

The names Child of God and Saint give us some idea.

A Personal New Name

Besides bestowing upon us *Child of God* and *Saint* as new names, God may have a personal new name for you especially, even as He did for Peter. What that name would be I cannot know. Your personal new name is God's name for you, not mine or someone else's. Of each overcoming Christian in Pergamum, Jesus said, "I will also give him a white stone with a new name written on it, known only to him who receives it" (Rev. 2:17).

I don't mean to be overly mystical or to insist that your first concern ought to be discovering some secret name God has for you. But I do feel certain that you need to exchange any bad name you have for a good one from God.

I did. Back around 1963, I felt stymied and frustrated, like I was at a dead end. Not that things were all bad. I had organized a country church six years or so earlier and had been its only pastor ever since. We had built our own building debt-free, had seen our numbers increase many fold, and had seen young people and others commit their lives fully to Christ. Some had gone into full-time Christian vocations.

I was driving a school bus part-time then to augment my meager salary. Sometimes I had to wait at the school awhile between loads, and I used that time to meditate and pray. As my unsettled state, my dissatisfaction, my feeling that I was stagnating grew, I spent a good deal of my waiting time wrestling with that problem.

I needed a word from God. Really, I needed a new name to replace the name *Dead End,* though I wasn't thinking in terms of names then. The passage of Scripture that became God's message to me at that time was Isaiah 62:3, "You will be a crown of splendor in the Lord's hand, a royal diadem in the hand of your God."

Those words may or may not seem very meaningful to you, but to me they became a source of new hope and courage. I wasn't through. I wasn't to stagnate in a backwater somewhere, forgotten by God. I was to be *a crown of splendor* in His hand. In the strength of that assurance, I moved forward.

Years passed before I realized what had happened, even though the context of "my verse" states it quite explicitly. "You will be called by a new name," says the preceding verse. "No longer will they call you Deserted," says the verse following "my verse." I had been given a new and encouraging name from God.

What about you? Should you change your name? No, not arbitrarily, just on your own. If you do that the new name may not stick. But you could talk the whole matter over with the Lord. He created you with many good things in mind and it only makes sense that He has a good name for you to go along with that plan.

Note

1. James D. Mallory, Jr. with Stanley C. Baldwin, *The Kink and I* (Wheaton, IL: Scripture Press Publications, 1973), p. 79.

PART III
The Put-Down Phenomenon: How and Why People Degrade Others

Chapter 8

Parents: They Bring You Up and Put You Down

Our daughter Krystal, her husband Bill, and their three little girls recently moved into a new neighborhood. I hesitate to call Bill and Krystal ideal parents, but they come about as close as any I know. They are sensitive and loving, yet firm. And they are keenly aware of the need to nurture their children's sense of worth.

Imagine Krystal's dismay, then, upon meeting a new neighbor, to hear the mother introduce her two-year-old son as Matt-brat.

Obviously this mother was not aware of the damaging effect a demeaning name can have on a child. Unfortunately, however, tacking unflattering nicknames on their children is only one way parents, who are supposed to bring their children up, often put them down. Another, and perhaps more common parental put-down, is the negative characterizing remark.

Dr. Honor Whitney of Texas Women's University surveyed thousands of men and women to discover how many remembered hearing certain put-down phrases from their parents.[1] Nine of every ten surveyed remembered hearing: "How many times do I have to tell you?"

Other common phrases that make children feel bad include:

- Do you expect me to believe that?
- Look at you—you're a mess.
- When are you going to grow up?
- Can't you do anything right?
- That was a stupid thing to do.
- I guess I just can't trust you.
- You are a bad boy (girl).

A slightly different type of parental put-down is the prophecy of failure:

- You'll never amount to anything.
- I pity you when you leave home.
- How do you ever hope to support a family?
- You'll never land a husband.

Then there is the unfavorable comparison type of put-down. "Look at this report card. You got a D in English again? Why can't you be like your brother Philip? He never gets below a B in anything."

Where there is no brother or sister with whom to compare a child, parents may cite their own example. "Why is it so hard to get you to do anything around the house? I always *wanted* to help my mother; she had to work so hard cleaning up after the whole family all the time."

So it goes. One way or another, parents often injure the self-esteem of their children.

Most parents, thank God, also build up their children in countless small but significant ways. Most important, they love their children and express that love by playing with them, praising their accomplishments, soothing their hurts, and listening to their childish prattle. Every such act on the part of a parent says: "You are important."

Think of the poor child, though, whose parents put him down constantly but never counter it by treating him with love and acceptance. The small child's whole world, virtually, is his home. If the feedback there is all demeaning, the child has little chance of emerging unscathed.

The emotional damage inflicted on such a child is frightening, as the following true account by a young woman graphically reveals:

"Why?" The question hung in the air as my 10-year-old brother shifted his weight from one foot to the other.

"Robby," Mother repeated, "why did you cause so much trouble at school again?"

"I don't know," he muttered. "I . . . I'm sorry."

"Well, I don't know either," Mother said. "I just don't understand you. I wish you'd show some appreciation for all I do. What does it take to satisfy you? Maybe we should send you to a reform school."

She went on and on, reviewing everything Robby had done wrong in his entire short life.

I could hear it all from my room, and I knew how Robby felt. I felt the same way. In this home so lacking in physical expressions of love, we two had drawn closer together than most brothers and sisters. We confided in each other, built up torn egos, and mended tattered feelings. We loved and protected each other from our formidable parent.

That we should fear and hate our own mother had never seemed strange to us. We grew up hating her. We were, in her words, "worthless, useless, clumsy, and unappreciative." We could do nothing right. We became excessively shy and unsure of ourselves. I chewed my fingernails until they bled and became infected. Robby became rebellious.

"Go to your room and stay there until supper!" I heard her shout at him at last.

Robby shut himself in his room. As soon as I could, I joined him.

"Go away," he said.

I tried to help. "It doesn't matter what she says, Rob. You're not that bad."

"Yes, I am," he said. "She's right. I'm no good. I can't do anything right. I shouldn't even be living." There was a strange frightening emptiness in his eyes. His voice sounded drained of emotion.

"Leave me alone," he said in a whisper.

Hurt and confused, I left him. I walked outdoors, through a wooded area behind our house. I had often walked out here when depressed. I would look at the sky and talk to God. I wanted to know Him, to feel His love.

We needed love so much. Mother was so impatient and exacting; she never smiled at us or hugged us. Dad was away so much on business that he didn't realize what was happening.

"God, You must care," I cried. "You've just got to." I stayed until Mother called.

I started back to the house. In the middle of the wooded area, a rustling in the trees caught my attention. I looked up and saw legs dangling through the leaves. My heart froze.

"Robby!" I screamed. I tore through the brush and climbed the tree. The branches and vines fought me, scratching at my face and arms. My fingernails began to bleed from my struggle with the heavy rope. It was thick, and the knot held, tightened by the weight of Robby's swaying body. Sweat ran down my forehead and stung my eyes.

"O God," I prayed. "If You care about us at all, help me. Please!"

Robby was no longer moving. I remembered the small jackknife he carried in his pocket. I searched, grasped it, and cut at the rope. Robby flopped to the ground. I scrambled down and cradled his head in my hands.

"Robby, Robby, please be all right!" I sobbed over and over. "You can't give up. God loves us. I know it. He helped me save you." I looked down at his face, and through blurry eyes saw him smile weakly at me.

"Do you really think so?" he asked, his voice raspy.

"Yes," I said. "He gave you another chance. Maybe we can get to know more about God. We could start going to that Sunday School on the hill."

"Mom will never take us," he said, crying.

"We can walk. It's not far."

With the help of some wonderful Sunday School teachers we gained some self-confidence. Our home life didn't change overnight. But God had begun to work. He never let up.[2]

Robby's story, no thanks to his parents, had a happy ending though his scars no doubt remain. How much different and better Robby's life might have been had his parents contributed to his sense of worth from the beginning.

As Jane Merchant's parents did.

Jane was born with *osteogenesis imperfecta*, a congenital bone disease causing the bones to fracture easily. Jane never walked, became bedfast at age 13, and lived as a "helpless invalid" for the next 40 years until her death in 1972. She was also deaf for the last 30 years of her life.

Not surprisingly, Jane struggled with her own sense of worth, but she came through in grand style. Her 2,000 poems blessed the lives of thousands, and though she never attended school, one of her fans, a professor at the University of Tennessee, spoke of her as the best educated mind he had ever encountered.

God's earliest provision for developing Jane's sense of worth was a pair of unusually wise and loving parents. They treated her consistently as a useful and unique member of the household. Thus, despite her own limitations and the low estate of her parents, who lost their farm to drought and the depression and lived on the edge of poverty most of their lives, Jane Merchant had a profound sense of her own worth.

She knew how essential self-respect is and how deadly self-pity is, and wrote of both in her poem "Purchase," which tells of a young man who, like her, was deaf.

> I almost bought a dozen combs today,
> A dozen combs I didn't need at all,
> Because the thin boy offering the array,
> At the back door, of various large and small
> Combs of all kinds and colors, when I said,
> "Good Morning," showed me, with a resolute
> White face, a narrow card on which I read
> The neatly lettered words, "I'm deaf and mute."

A thrush was singing then. I would have bought
His whole supply, but that his look forbade
My charity; so after careful thought
I took just one, the finest one he had.
I could not sleep tonight if I had tried
To buy his courage of him, and his pride.[3]

Jesus said we must take heed to the little ones for they have a special place in the heart of the Father.[4] Part of our responsibility surely is that we build up, not destroy, their sense of value as human beings. God says they *are special*, and woe to us if we convince them they are not.

Notes

1. Reported in *Woman's Day*, September 20, 1977. "How to Give and Get More Emotional Support" by Norman M. Lobsenz, pp. 73,148,150.
2. Adapted by permission from *Free Way* (Wheaton, IL: Scripture Press Publications, Inc., 1973).
3. Jane Merchant, "Purchase," *The Greatest of These* (Nashville: Abingdon Press, © 1954). Used by permission.
4. See Matthew 18:1-10.

Chapter 9

Put-Downs, Put-downs, Everywhere Put-downs

A child fortunate enough to have sensitive, loving parents who never put him down is truly blessed. Even so, he will not venture far beyond the circle of his immediate family before he is put down by other people.

The put-down may be very blunt. "Go away; we don't like you." Or it may be subtle but still unmistakably real and cruel.

Certainly when a youngster reaches school age if not before, he will be victimized by that cruel childhood practice of choosing up sides. You know how it works. The gang is going to play ball and teams must be organized. Captains are designated, often by popular agreement. Then the captains set in motion a procedure that can only end in the humiliation of some of the children.

The captains choose players in order of (1) how well they think you can play the game, (2) how well they happen to like you.

If you can't play the game well and if you are not

particularly liked, you are in trouble. And if you happen to be the least "choosable" of all, you are in big trouble. You are going to be put down openly, before everyone else in the group. It's almost as if you are on display and the word is being announced: "Look, everybody, this person is the least among us, the bottom of the heap, worthless."

Being thus shamed by one's peers can be an agonizing experience. However, for some children, especially smaller ones, it's even worse to be put down by an authority figure such as a teacher. Yet, though this can be a terribly damaging thing, it is also a rather common one.

Levauna Smith, my sister, tells how she was turned off to school and wounded emotionally by an insensitive teacher. She was in fourth grade when the teacher walked the aisles one day observing the children at work coloring pictures. When she reached Levauna's desk, she asked critically, "Where did you ever learn to color sky?"

Levauna took the question quite literally and replied, "At Kenwood," the school she had attended the year before. The whole class laughed, and Levauna gathered that she was not only stupid for answering as she had but for coloring sky badly, though she never did know what was wrong—she used blue.

Some time later the same teacher ridiculed her for saying that Old Ironsides was called that because it was an iron ship. Again the teacher and the other students laughed at her. If the teacher ever told her what was wrong with her answer, Levauna didn't hear it. She was too embarrassed and humiliated.

From then on, though she had been a good student before, Levauna withdrew into a shell. She never volunteered an answer, and if the teacher asked her a question she simply said she didn't know. She failed the fourth grade and never did well in school again.

The teacher had literally destroyed her self-esteem, had made her feel "dumb and ugly and worthless," and had so marred her life that it took her the next 20 years to get over it.

Probably most people could tell of somewhat similar experiences, though not so damaging in their effect, one would hope. Certainly I can recall a few unpleasant incidents from my own school days.

One that stands out in my mind occurred when I was in fifth grade. I was supposed to carry a placard in a school program. From onstage center, I was to slip out front between the great stage curtains at just the right time. At rehearsal I failed to appear on cue once or twice simply because I couldn't see where the curtains parted. I told the teacher so, but she seemed to think I must be pretty stupid. "Stand right here," she told me impatiently as she positioned me directly behind the center of the curtain.

I stood there, listening intently for my cue. I wanted so badly to do what I was supposed to and not make Mrs. Green angry. When I knew it was time, I attacked the curtain, hoping the invisible opening would indeed be there. It was, but the heavy material caught both sides of my placard and I couldn't get through.

Mrs. Green was on me at once. "What happened *this* time?" she demanded.

"I couldn't get through," I replied. "My card's too wide."

"Well, of course you can't just shove it through right straight ahead," she said, as if I were the dumbest person she had ever seen. She took the placard from my hands. "You have to turn it sideways and slip it through," she said. "Like this."

She could have done worse, I suppose. She could have taken the assignment away from me and given it to another child who would make it look easy. But the disdainful manner in which she corrected me made the effect almost as bad as if she had rejected me completely.

Later that same year I also ran afoul of my art teacher. She told everyone in my class to cut out a picture of a ship from a calendar or magazine and bring it to school. "Don't tell me you can't find one," she said. "I'm sure you can if you look."

We had no magazines at our house and no calendars with a picture of a ship. Since the teacher had already said she wouldn't accept excuses, I saw no choice but to simply fail the assignment.

When I showed up minus a ship, the teacher was upset. "That's why you Baldwin kids always fail," she stormed at me in front of the whole class. "You just don't try."

That was too much. I took considerable pride in my good report cards and I didn't care to be lumped in with others in the family who supposedly did not. I had to challenge her statement. "I never got a failing grade in my life!" I protested.

"Well, you *will* next report period," she said.

Sure enough, my next report card showed a failing grade in art. My homeroom teacher was Mrs. Rubeneck, and you can guess what the kids called her. "Mrs. Rubberneck" had a reputation for being tough, but she and I always got along fine. When she saw my grade in art, she asked what had happened. I told her, "The art teacher has it in for me."

"Oh, no, I'm sure that's not true," Mrs. Rubeneck said. "I'll have a talk with her."

Through Mrs. Rubeneck's good offices, the art teacher learned I was not a negligent student. Her attitude toward me changed entirely and my art grade bounced right back up.

I had dodged the bullet. "Stupid" was not to become one of the bad names I would later have to shed.

Grown-Ups Get Put Down Too

Even when they leave childhood behind, people continue to receive in countless ways the message:

- You are not important.
- You are not acceptable.
- You are not desirable.
- You do not measure up.

Maybe we are not invited when others get together for a party or activity. Maybe our opinions are not sought when an issue is being discussed. If we volunteer our views we may be ignored.

Some put-downs are extremely subtle and quite unintentional. I cringed inside when I heard a pastor pray for a couple of teenage boys who had responded to his invitation to step forward for Christ after his sermon. He prayed that God would bless "Bob and his friend" as they made this important decision.

Bob and *his friend*? Even before God was this young man with Bob nobody in his own right? Did he only count as a friend of somebody else? Somebody named Bob who was important enough to be recognized?

I was sure the pastor hadn't meant to slight the

young man. Apparently he simply did not know his name. Maybe the young man didn't even notice. Still, it was a put-down, however subtle and unintentioned. Along with a multitude of other personal put-downs of various kinds, it might well have added its small weight of self-reproach.

Put-downs do indeed come in many forms. We spoke in the previous chapter about *parental* put-downs. Before that, in the chapter on our new names, we talked about *propositional* put-downs—using theological propositions about the sinfulness of man to unduly beat down believers who should have moved from a sinner identity to that of saint.

So far in this chapter, we've described *peer* put-downs among children, *patronistic* put-downs by teachers, and *personal* put-downs that can come to us at any age and from anyone. We need now to give particular attention to what we will call *possessional* and *positional* put-downs.

Possessional Put-downs

Our possessions can cause us definite self-esteem problems. I'm not talking only about not being able to wear such nice clothes as others, not being able to drive such a fine car, or not living in so lavish a house. All those possessional shortfalls certainly can damage self-esteem.

However, even if you live on a par with those around you, your possessions can still cause you serious trouble. You see, every time anyone puts down something you own, your self-esteem comes under assault. The very fact that you possess an item suggests you want it or find it acceptable. Therefore, if someone else puts it down, he is saying something is wrong with you. Your judgment or your taste or your ability to provide for yourself is not very good. A more subtle message is that you are inferior to the one who is criticizing you.

The practice of putting down other people's possessions is a bad one. Unfortunately, some people do it constantly. I described such a person in my book *What Makes You So Special*?

> I knew a woman like that once. Whatever we had, she put it down. When we got a piece of furniture, she said it was "nice, but I wouldn't want it because that fabric tends to frizz and the store where you bought it sells inferior merchandise." If we got a new car, it was wonderful, but she wouldn't want it because those vinyl seats are so hot in summertime. Besides, she knew so and so who had one like it and had nothing but trouble.[1]

Why are we often inclined to behave like that woman? Why do we have to add our little "but" phrases when we say something nice? It has been correctly observed that any time we make such a "but" statement, the but effectively cancels everything that went before it so far as the emotional impact on the other person is concerned. The "nice" comment is nullified completely and the "but" remark is all that remains.

Suppose I said to you, "Friend, you are nice looking but you really are not wearing your hair right for the shape of your face." What would you carry away from that encounter? Would you go away feeling good and saying to yourself, "He thinks I am nice looking"?

Hardly. You would go away thinking, *Ohhhh,*

he doesn't like my hairstyle. It must be really bad.

It's important to understand what's going on behind the scenes in a situation like this. Such understanding may help us stop injuring other people as well as spare us unnecessary injury at their hands.

To help explain the dynamics of such an exchange between people, let me tell you about my brother's car purchase some time ago. "I got this great deal on a Chrysler," Ron told me. "Only cost me $800 and it's in wonderful shape. You've got to see it."

The first thing I noticed about the Chrysler was that the left front fender was a slightly different shade of green than the rest of the car. That meant one thing. The car had been in an accident and the left front fender had been repainted.

My inclination was to point this fact out to Ron, to say something like, "It's really nice, *but* it has been in an accident."

I resisted the temptation. Instead I commented honestly on how beautiful the interior was, how good the general condition of the car seemed, and what a good buy it was.

If I had mentioned the fender, what would have been my reason? I mean, he had already bought the car. Beneath the surface I would have been saying in effect, "Hey, I'm a very wise and observant person. I noticed something right away that you overlooked. I not only noticed it but I know what it means. What's the matter with you, you poor dummy?"

The bottom line of such communication is: "I'm smart and you are not."

The probable reason I would say such a thing is

that I have some difficulty with my own self-image. As a result, I need to extract some good feelings about myself whenever and however I can. So I do it at his expense.

Why can't we just give a gift? Why can't we just say it's nice, period? The inability to do so is a dead giveaway that we are not whole.

Jesus said, "Freely you have received, freely give" (Matt. 10:8). When we have received the emotional wholeness Jesus wants to give us, then we will be able to give freely to other people with no "buts" attached.

I'm sometimes asked, "But what if a negative statement needs to be made. Suppose instead of the mismatched paint, you had discovered the brakes were faulty. What then? Would you still just say nice things so the other person would feel good?"

No. The error on one side is to put people down because we have problems of our own. The error on the other side is to be dishonest or even destructive in the name of being nice.

If I notice that the brake pedal very slowly gives under continued foot pressure, I still don't have to say, "It's nice, *but* . . ." I can say, "It's nice, *and* even though I think there may be a small problem with the brakes, that is a relatively minor expense, especially considering the great buy you made."

Positional Put-downs

Closely related to the possessional put-down is the positional put-down. Just as your possessions represent you, so do your positions on political and religious matters. To some degree, your position on any issue is an extension of you.

Thus, when people put down your position,

they detract from you as a person. It is certainly appropriate to differ on issues without attacking the other person. Often, however, people put down the view that conflicts with their own as if it were ridiculous and no right-thinking person could possibly hold it. The one being subjected to this treatment senses, correctly, that he is being put down.

Dr. James D. Mallory, Jr. gives an example of this kind of interaction in his book *The Kink and I*:

> I got caught up in this one time in a conversation at a Christian Medical Society meeting. Two visiting freshmen began to reel off a lot of the statements that you will hear sometimes about Christianity being myth and about how man has learned all these new things that pretty well explode the outmoded concepts of the Bible. My reaction to these men was not exactly compassionate. They were coming across as confident in their "new" knowledge that was supposed to show us Christians we were all wrong.
>
> My ego response was, *Who do these two think they are? I worked through all that intellectual ego-trip years ago. I know better than that. They act as if they've got something new to tell me.* My ego was being threatened; they were implying I was not as smart as they. So I began to put them down, to point out that their line of thinking wasn't all that logical.
>
> I had a flash of insight in the midst of

> this encounter that I was winning this battle but losing these two young men. It was an agonizing thing to realize that my witness was really an expression of my hostility. I was rejecting these fellows and puffing up my own ego.[2]

Dr. Mallory realized he was putting down these two young men, not just differing with them. The fact is, though, they had put him down first by the manner in which they spoke about Christian faith.

When you have everyone fighting for his own self-respect like that, no learning is likely to take place. Positions are hardened and hostilities become entrenched. By contrast, when our faith is genuinely strong and we are emotionally whole, we are not easily threatened or disturbed by others' expressions of unbelief and we can then witness to them effectively. We may even learn a few things ourselves in the process.

We have discussed various put-downs at length for two reasons. First, you need to recognize what has gone into the formation of your personal self-image. If you have suffered from low self-esteem, you should better understand now why that has been so.

The second reason we've gone on at some length about put-downs is that you need to realize the damage you can do to others unintentionally. There is no assurance that knowing will help you do better. Those who put down others usually do so because of unsatisfied needs in their own lives. Simply reading a damage assessment is not likely to change their behavior, because it leaves the needs unsatisfied.

Still, if you are a Christian, the knowledge that

you are injuring others certainly ought to add urgency to your desire to get a true view of you. For you will go on suffering and you will go on injuring others until you do.

The good news is that help for your self-esteem problem is not hard to find. It may be hard to appropriate for it requires that you learn new ways of thinking. Replacing bad habits with good ones takes time, and that applies to mental habits as much as any others. That's all the more reason to begin in earnest right now.

Memorize some of the great biblical texts that reveal how you ought to view yourself: Ephesians 1:6; 1 Corinthians 4:7; Genesis 1:27; Psalm 8:5; Luke 12:6,7; Jeremiah 29:11; Psalm 139:17,18; 1 John 3:1; Ephesians 1:18; Jude 24.

Select a verse from this list that is particularly helpful to you, memorize it, claim it, live by it. Make it your verse. Or appropriate them all. Yes, it will take some effort, but your self-esteem is at stake here. You need to be transformed by a renewed mind, a reprogrammed mind, a mind that thinks God's thoughts. That won't happen all by itself, but *it can happen.*

Will it happen to you?

Notes

1. Stanley C. Baldwin, *What Makes You So Special?* (Grand Rapids: Baker Book House, 1977), pp. 41,42.
2. James D. Mallory with Stanley C. Baldwin, *The Kink and I* (Wheaton, IL: Scripture Press Publications, Inc., 1973), pp. 179,180.

PART IV
Failure Isn't Fatal—Necessarily

Chapter 10

Sin: Failing the Lord

Two major causes of low self-esteem combine to harass most people. The first, put-downs from without, was the subject of the previous section. A second and related problem comes from within. It is a sense of personal failure.

One of the most degrading failures we experience is *sinning.* Our sins are ours alone. Even so, the effect of our sinning is often related to how others react to our sin. Sometimes people are more influenced by the attitudes of others toward their wrongdoing than by the wrongdoing itself.

What Will People Think?

The story is told of a small western town that suddenly experienced a mass exodus of some of its leading citizens. Practically overnight several families packed up their belongings and moved away. It was all quite mysterious.

Then the truth came out. A prankster had sent identical anonymous letters all over town. The letters said: "The jig is up. By week's end everyone will know exactly what you have done."[1]

Now, I ask you, did the letters really change anything? They certainly didn't affect the guilt or innocence of the recipients. They only caused those who had done wrong to become acutely aware of it and to contemplate the effect of exposure. This moved them to drastic action.

Let's get the picture clearly.

The citizens in our little story were comfortably interacting with each other day by day—holding their heads high, looking one another in the eye, treating one another as equals—until the exposé threatened. Then everything changed. Everything, that is, except their true guilt. It was exactly the same after the letters were sent as before. You see, our guilt feelings often relate to how we think others will judge our behavior.

Sin Offends God, but Feeling Guilty Is What Bothers Us

A TV news magazine show was doing a story about a con man and the way he had bilked people out of their hard-earned savings. One of the victims commented about the con man, "I'm sure he doesn't sleep very well at night."

The next scene showed the newsman interviewing the offender, who freely admitted being unethical in his dealings. When asked how well he slept nights, the man answered with all seeming candor, "I sleep just fine."

Guilt doesn't seem to bother some people very much. Let me go further and suggest what may sound radical at first: *the fact of our own wrongdoing seldom bothers any of us.*

"That cannot be," someone protests. "Don't

psychologists speak at great lengths about the severely damaging effects of guilt? They say guilt breeds fear because we anticipate getting our just reward. It leads to accidents and illnesses because we so strongly feel we should be punished that we subconsciously punish ourselves. It makes us suspicious and worried and unhappy. And it devastates our self-esteem."

Someone else says, "Not bothered? I could tell you stories that would make you cry about the pangs of suffering brought on by a guilty conscience."

Yet a third person might say, "Read the Scriptures. Read how David suffered intensely when he was covering up his great sin with Bathsheba."

The Prodigal Son could be cited in further refutation of my radical statement. He linked guilt to a sense of unworthiness in the speech he prepared upon his return to his father. "I will . . . say to him: Father, I have sinned against heaven and against you. I am no longer worthy to be called your son" (Luke 15:18,19). Does not the conviction "I've sinned" lead directly, then, to the feeling "I am not worthy"?

Ah, yes, but there has been a subtle switch here. Did you notice it? The radical statement had to do with the *fact* of our wrongdoing but the examples had to do with a *conviction* of that wrongdoing, and there is a huge difference.

The problem is that the word *guilt* is imprecise in its meaning. The first definition in *Webster's* is "the fact of having committed a breach of conduct." This is what I've been calling "the fact of our wrongdoing." The second definition for guilt is "culpability," and the third is "a feeling of culpability for offenses."

You see, then, that the word guilt does not differentiate between the *fact* and the *feeling*, between the actual wrongdoing and the feeling of being to blame.

This seems unfortunate because it can foul up our thinking on this subject. There is a great practical difference between wrongdoing and self-blame.

The Prodigal Son, for instance, was guilty in fact when he rejected his father and all he stood for and went off to seek his own selfish ends. He was guilty in fact when he wasted his substance in wild living. But we heard no "I-am-not-worthy" speeches from him then. Nothing in the story remotely hints that any twinges of conscience marred his good time. Only after he was bearing the consequences of his choices and indeed, as the account goes, only after he "came to his senses" (Luke 15:17) did his wrongdoing seriously bother him.

King David too apparently continued for months after his adultery with Bathsheba and murder of Uriah before he experienced the guilt feelings he describes in Psalm 32: "When I kept silent, my bones wasted away through my groaning all day long. For day and night your hand was heavy upon me; my strength was sapped as in the heat of summer" (vv. 3,4).

Some imagine that this psalm describes David's frame of mind all during the months before his sin was exposed. I think not. David had quite successfully glossed over his wrongdoing, not only with the public but in his own heart. That is why God sent the prophet Nathan with his parable of the rich man who stole his neighbor's pet lamb and made a meal of it. There was a need to arouse David's conscience, to make him *feel* his guilt.

"What a Wretch I Am"

Both David and the Prodigal Son needed to feel guilty in order to be moved to repentance. That is the proper role of guilt feelings in our lives too. Unfortunately, guilt feelings are often used by Satan for destructive ends instead.

Guilt made the Prodigal Son feel unworthy, but not so unworthy that he stayed where he was. He arose and went to his father. "But while he was still a long way off, his father saw him and was filled with compassion for him; he ran to his son, threw his arms around him and kissed him" (Luke 15:20).

The father proceeded to give the prodigal a royal welcome that left no doubt how much he esteemed him. Jesus told the story to illustrate how God feels toward those who repent after being alienated from Him by sin. The trouble is that God doesn't get a chance to welcome sinners so royally if they feel like such failures that they won't come near Him.

The sin problem also troubles the Christian who already has come to God for forgiveness and eternal life but finds he still does wrong. That was Paul's situation at one time. The description of his inner state shows how devastating to his sense of worth it was. "I have the desire to do what is good, but I cannot carry it out. For what I do is not the good I want to do; no, the evil I do not want to do—this I keep on doing. . . . What a wretched man I am!" (Rom. 7:18,19,24).

For such a distressed person, even the forgiveness of God can be distorted to make things seem worse instead of better. The person asks God to forgive him, sincerely regrets his transgression, and vows not to do it again. But he does.

As this pattern continues, he becomes more and more disgusted with himself. He comes to God with even more sorrow, and works up more determination than ever that "this time" he will not fail again. But again he does. Eventually, the "wretched-man-that-I-am" cry of Paul becomes his as well. He is trapped with a terrible self-image.

Good Repentance Versus Bad Repentance

Of course, such a person as we have been describing needs to overcome his habitual sin. It seems clear, however, that he will not do so by continuing his present pattern of behavior. It simply is not working.

What he needs is to know that he is not condemned, however rotten he feels, and that God will give him the strength to live differently (see Rom. 8:1-4). This assurance eludes him so long as he has a fixation on his sin.

We read, "Those who live according to their sinful nature have their minds set on what that nature desires; but those who live in accordance with the Spirit have their minds set on what the Spirit desires" (Rom. 8:5).

You see, even his repentance, sincere as it is, tends to set the mind of the defeated Christian on his sinful nature and what it desires. Unfortunately, some church fellowships are sin-oriented in much the same way. They have a tremendous emphasis on the world, the flesh, and the devil, and then wonder why they have trouble with all three constantly.

What is the solution? To stop repenting? No, but to repent after a godly fashion. The Bible talks about a repentance that doesn't need to be repented of, implying that there is both a wrong kind of repentance and a right kind (see 2 Cor. 7:10).

The contrast between bad and good repentance is well explained by Bruce Narramore and Bill Counts under the terms "psychological guilt" and "constructive sorrow."

> Psychological guilt and constructive sorrow are very different feelings. Psychological guilt is largely self-centered. Its real concern is not, "What have I done to others and how can I correct the harm I have done them?" Instead, it focuses on: "What a failure *I* am"; "What will everyone think of *me*?" or "*I* am no good." Adam and Eve apparently didn't have the slightest concern that they had plunged the world into rebellion and thrown a monkey wrench into God's plan for the universe. They were just afraid they would be punished—one form of guilt.
>
> Guilt focuses largely on our past failures, our sense of wrongdoing, and our feelings of deserving punishment. In short, it looks largely at ourselves and at our failures. Constructive sorrow focuses more on the persons we have injured. It is a very deep feeling but is not as concerned with our own failures as it is the damage done to others.

Narramore and Counts sum up the difference best, perhaps, in the following passage:

> *Psychological guilt produces self-*

> *inflicted misery. Constructive sorrow produces a positive change of behavior.* Once the change in behavior comes, constructive sorrow vanishes. Its purpose is accomplished.[2]

This analysis reminds one of Alfred Adler's statement, "Those who feel guilty have no intention of changing." Feeling guilty can be a substitute for true repentance. It is a way of punishing ourselves for wrongdoing instead of stopping the behavior. On the other hand, those who have sincerely repented have no need to feel guilty. They have been forgiven for past sins and do not expect to continue them in the future.

When one repents, then, he must turn from the sin and from the sorrow over it to the new way of living that God intends for us. He must get his mind "set on what the Spirit desires."

As Paul put it after leaving his "wretched-man-that-I-am" days behind, "Do not be overcome by evil, but overcome evil with good" (Rom. 12:21).

That's it!

Do you see?

Sin is to be crowded out, not by focusing upon it but by replacing it with good. The same principle for living underlies the familiar words, "Do not conform any longer to the pattern of this world, but be transformed by the renewing of your mind" (Rom. 12:2). In both passages, God's "do not" is followed by "do," and it is the do that holds the secret of successfully following through on the do not.

Those who focus on nonconformity to the world fight a losing battle, often against shadows, because they have no adequate basis for being transformed. But those who are transformed by a renewed mind are also, by that very process, safeguarded against being conformed any longer to the world.

When we sin, we should see such behavior as uncharacteristic of us, not as proof that we are no good. Sin is a holdover from our old life which, Scripture teaches, is to be viewed as crucified, dead, and buried with Christ (see Rom. 6:1-6). We are new people, called to a better and higher way, and it is this new way of the Spirit that must come to occupy our attention.[3]

Because guilt feelings are so damaging to self-esteem and to the personality, Christian psychologists and writers have suggested various ways of handling them. You may find some of their suggestions helpful.

Recognize False Guilt

Can a person feel guilty without being guilty in fact?

Yes.

On May 28, 1977, a fire raged through the Beverly Hills Supper Club near Cincinnati, Ohio. It took the lives of 164 people including a young married couple named Paula and Elliott Neill, Jr. Paula would not have been there that night if her parents had not declined her invitation for them to spend the evening at her home. Because they did she had gone to the club instead where her husband worked as a drummer. After she died her parents said they had "such a guilt load that it's hard to bear."

They weren't the only ones. Cincinnati General Central Psychiatric Clinic reported that patrons who survived the fire, rescue workers, and employees of the club were also experiencing guilt feelings, though they were in no way to blame for the deaths.

Dr. James Dobson describes the guilt of parents who produce defective children as an example of unjustified guilt. He writes:

> A sense of guilt sweeps over some parents in such enormous quantities that the family is destroyed by its impact. Now, it is obvious that God is not the author of this kind of disapproval. He knows—even better than we—that the grief-stricken parents did not intentionally produce a defective child. Their genetic system simply malfunctioned. Certainly our merciful Creator would not hold them responsible for a consequence which they could not have anticipated or avoided. Nevertheless, the guilt is often unbearable for parents who hold *themselves* personally responsible.[4]

Bruce Narramore and Bill Counts explain false guilt this way:

> The first question we should ask ourselves when we feel a tinge of guilt is, "*Did I really blow it?*" In other words, we want to determine if we really did something wrong or if we only violated the childish standards of our ideal self—our inner parent. Most of us feel guilty over a number of things God doesn't consider sin.
>
> I often encounter college students whose parents are absolutely determined their children get their college degrees. Sometime during their college years the students wake up to the fact they don't

want to be in college. They would prefer to marry or enter a vocation that doesn't require college education. Yet as soon as they consider "dropping out" they start feeling guilty. They're afraid they're letting their parents down. Later if they do drop out, they may repeatedly be haunted by the thought that they made the wrong decision. When a girl in this situation marries, she often starts resenting her husband for "depriving her of an education or profession."

In similar ways, we all feel guilty over some less-than-perfect ideals. Some men feel guilty if they aren't working all the time. Some women feel guilty if their homes aren't spotless. Some of us feel guilty if we have nice things, and others feel guilty if we don't. Still others feel guilty if they don't say yes to every request to serve in their church or social organization.

But the Bible doesn't say every American should get a college degree, have a spotless home, teach a Sunday school class or work sixteen hours a day. Many people who battle guilt are not doing wrong; they are condemning themselves for failing to live up to their ideal self—the borrowed standards of their parents or society.[5]

How do you deal with false guilt?

Basically, you do it by believing God instead of your condemning conscience. If you have resolved some question of right or wrong by consulting God, if He has given approval to your course of action, you say to your conscience, "You are wrong, and I am not going to listen to your accusations."

As the Scripture says, "Whenever our conscience condemns us, God is greater than our conscience and knows everything" (1 John 3:20, Beck).

Judge Yourself by Your Intent

Dr. James Dobson says, "I personally believe no guilt should be considered to have come from God unless the behavior was an expression of willful disobedience." He cites an example of his small son misunderstanding an order and doing the opposite of what was commanded. He excuses that, and says, "You see, I judge my son more by his *intent* than by his actual behavior. . . . It is with great comfort that I rest in that same relationship with God."

Dr. Dobson gives the following example:

> One mother whom I know walked toward a busy street with her three-year-old daughter. The little toddler ran ahead and stopped on the curb until her mother told her it was safe to cross. The woman was thinking about something else and nodded in approval when the little child asked, "Can I go now, Mommy?"
>
> The youngster ran into the street and was struck full force by a semi-trailer truck. The mother gasped in terror as she watched the front and back wheels of the truck crush the life from her precious little girl. The hysterical woman, screaming in anguish and grief, ran to the road and gathered the broken remains of the

> child in her arms. She had killed her own daughter who depended on her for safety. This mother will *never* escape the guilt of that moment. The "video tape recording" has been rerun a million times in her tormented mind—picturing a trusting baby asking her mother if it was safe to cross the street. Clearly, God has not placed that guilt on the heartbroken woman, but her suffering is no less real.[6]

With all due compassion for this woman, and granting that her intentions were good, one might ask whether she was not to some degree to blame for not exercising more care.

Thus, it is not clear how helpful it is to say that true guilt only attaches to those acts prompted by an evil intent. Clearly, to do wrong intentionally is worse than to do wrong inadvertently. However, there is a much more effective way to deal with guilt, a way that does not depend on such dubious distinctions.

Move Beyond Guilt

Almost in contradiction to Dr. Dobson's words are the following from Narramore and Counts:

> We may think only "conscious" faults are serious enough to attract God's attention or offend his holy nature. If sin is on the unconscious level, we suppose it's not so bad and can't separate us from him. Yet there is no hint in the Bible that wrongs must be "conscious" to be sin. This misunderstanding arises from a confusion of our human perspective and God's divine viewpoint. We know, of course, that some human failures have

especially bad effects on people. We know that some people are more openly rebellious. And we know that sometimes we are "better" than at others. But God doesn't fellowship with us on the basis of our good intentions, honest efforts, or "spirituality." He accepts us only on the basis of his character that demands one hundred percent perfection. Even an unconscious fault, while not seeming bad from our perspective, offends God and is sufficient to alienate us from him. The vital issue in terms of our relationship with God is *not* how hard we try, how *good* we are, or how *close* we come, but whether we have the one hundred percent righteousness God demands. If we do, we are acceptable to him; if we do not, we are *never* acceptable no matter how hard we try or how good and moral we may be. . . .

Even if we could avoid all negative sins, we would still have to be totally loving, completely forgiving, always thankful, and never worrying if we were to live up to God's standards and merit his daily approval.

Obviously, these standards are impossibly high. By seeing just how high they are, it should be clear that no one can keep them all. Therefore, the most mature Christian in the world with no conscious failings is not one bit more acceptable to God at any moment than we are at our worst moments or than the most rebellious Christian.

> There never has been any man—except Jesus Christ—who kept the law of God in its totality for even one day. If our daily acceptance by God were based on reaching these standards, every Christian should feel continually rejected.[7]

Supporting this view is James 2:10, which reads, "For whoever keeps the whole law and yet stumbles at just one point is guilty of breaking all of it."

This may sound like a more severe view than Dobson's. In a way it is. It says we *are guilty*. However, if we are Christians *our guilt is gone*.

As Narramore and Counts put it, "The New Testament clearly reveals . . . that all sins, past, present, and future are forgiven once and for all through the atonement of Christ. When we accept Christ, we obtain all the forgiveness we ever need."[8]

Or as the apostle Paul puts it, "Therefore, there is now no condemnation for those who are in Christ Jesus" (Rom. 8:1).

As believers we are in a truly enviable position regarding guilt. Because of Christ we stand free in the presence of God and man alike.

Nowhere is this pictured more clearly than in the account in John 8 of the woman taken in adultery. There was no question of her guilt for she was caught in the very act. What did Jesus say when confronted with this sinful woman by her accusers? He told them, "If any one of you is without sin, let him be the first to throw a stone at her" (v. 7).

We read, "At this, those who heard began to go away one at a time, the older ones first" (v. 9). I've always wondered about that. Why the older ones first? I don't know whether they were "dirty old men" and more guilty than the younger ones or whether they were just quicker to acknowledge their own guilt. Maybe it was both.

In any case, when they had all gone, Jesus said, "Woman, where are they? Has no one condemned you?"

"No one, sir," she said.

"Then neither do I condemn you," Jesus declared. "Go now and leave your life of sin" (vv. 10-12).

We, like this woman, are guilty without a doubt when our lives are stacked against the perfect demands of God's law. Yet no man is qualified to condemn us for they all are as surely guilty as we are. That leaves us standing before Jesus alone. And what does He say? "Neither do I condemn you."

Praise God! Man *cannot* condemn us, and the Lord *will not*, so we are free.

Someone may object that this gives a license to sin. No, Jesus says to us as He said to her, "Go now and leave your life of sin" (v. 11).

Did she?

Will we?

Yes.

We still won't be perfect, of course, but we will be free. Free from the driven, confused, sin-centered existence that has been our downfall all along until now. Free to begin living out the new life in the Spirit that we obviously wanted when we sincerely repented and promised God we would do His will. Free to know we aren't wretches.

We are beloved sons who have come home.

Notes

1. Adapted from Dale Galloway's *How to Feel Like a Somebody Again* (Eugene, OR: Harvest House Publishers, 1978).
2. Bruce Narramore and Bill Counts, *Guilt and Freedom* (Santa Ana, CA: Vision House Publishers), pp. 124, 125.
3. For an in-depth theological treatment of this theme see David C. Needham, *Birthright* (Portland, OR: Multnomah Press).
4. Dr. James Dobson, *Emotions: Can You Trust Them?* (Ventura, CA: Regal Books, 1980), p. 21.
5. Narramore and Counts, *Guilt and Freedom*, pp. 119, 120.
6. Dobson, *Emotions*, p.22.
7. Narramore and Counts, *Guilt and Freedom*, pp. 79-81.
8. Ibid.

Chapter 11

Frustration: Failing in Our Endeavors

Sin is one form of failure that can seriously damage our self-esteem, but it is by no means the only one. We may fail in an endeavor and be totally innocent of any wrongdoing. We *know* we haven't sinned. Yet we feel disgusted with ourselves just because we attempted something and it didn't turn out as we hoped. We failed.

Such experiences are not exclusive to incompetent people. They are common to all who aspire to achievement of any kind. Experiencing failure is part of the price of *doing* and can only be avoided by a profound withdrawal that is tantamount to resigning from life. And that, of course, is the biggest failure of all.

Some failures are more crucial than others and have more far-reaching effects, but all failure hurts. In this chapter and the next, we'll consider the damage to self-esteem that results from "little failures" and "big failures" and try to suggest some help for both.

Little Failures—Big Wounds

Craig Selness tells the following story of a failure he experienced as a boy:

> When I was in grade school, I was the captain of our spelling team. While I'm sure we won our share of spelling bees, the only one I remember distinctly is one we lost—or more accurately, the one I lost (at least that's how I felt).
>
> Our class was having a spelling bee against another class down the hall. My teacher and my classmates were all counting on me, their champion speller, to lead them to glorious victory.
>
> But early in the game, I choked. The teacher asked me to spell *prophet*, like the ones in the Bible. But the only word I could picture in my mind was spelled p-r-o-f-i-t. The teacher was so sure I could get it right that even after I spelled it wrong the first time she gave me another chance.
>
> I felt my classmates looking at me. I carried their hopes for victory in this all-important spelling bee. But the right letters wouldn't come. To the groans of my classmates, the loud cheers of the other team, and the obvious disappointment of my teacher who had such high expectations of me, I had failed. I had let them down.
>
> I ran to my desk and buried my head in my arms, tears streaking my face. It was a wound that hurt deeply and which took a long time to heal.[1]

The story illustrates how even a good student

can fail and feel worthless as a result. What about the poor student, then, the one who has to contend with failure regularly? He has just that much more to overcome.

A child may get poor grades because of a learning disability, a hearing or vision problem, or for some other reason that's not his fault. Still, because he hasn't performed well, he is likely to feel unworthy and unacceptable.

Some children are mislabeled "poor student" simply because they have gotten crossways of the system at some point, like Levauna, whose experience was described in chapter 9. Having failed conspicuously somewhere along the line, they are now identified as failures both by others and by themselves.

Some amazing things have happened when "poor students" have been placed under the influence of teachers who expected something better of them. In one case, a group of "slow learners" was assigned to a teacher who was told they were all exceptionally bright though somewhat eccentric. Because she thought they were above-average students she treated them that way. Every child soon showed marked improvement and many turned out to be quite capable students.

This phenomenon suggests one remedy for low self-esteem caused by failure. We need . . .

Somebody to Believe in Us

We are often caught in a vicious circle. We fail. As a result, people downgrade us, our confidence is destroyed, and our self-esteem is damaged. This in turn keeps us from attempting other things or causes us to try halfheartedly or predisposes us to expect to fail again.

But if someone believes in us we are encouraged to believe in ourselves as well. Unfortunately, finding people who will believe in you when you are "a failure" is not easy. Often mothers believe in us, but we tend to discount their belief in us as unjustified.

I have good news.

Somebody does believe in you.

It is the very one who has asked you to believe in Him.

God believes in you.

He made you and He endowed you with whatever capabilities and potential you have. How you compare with the other people He made and endowed doesn't matter, for He only expects performance from you commensurate with your endowments.

Would a just God create you incapable of flying and then reproach you because you can't fly? No. But He would be displeased with you if you could walk but won't. I say He'd be displeased, but His displeasure would largely be over *what you are missing* in life when you won't walk. He wants us to live abundantly.

The point is that God did not make you to be beat down by failure. If the limits on your ability are from Him, accept them and accept yourself as He does. If they are not from Him but are imposed on you because of past failure, remember that He believes in you because He knows what is possible for you. He's just waiting for you to shake off your self-pity and your unbelief and start moving.

It has been well said that failure is a word describing an event, not a person. You may have failed, but that doesn't mean you are a failure. Though a particular course or undertaking of yours failed, *you* are still a beautiful creation of God.

We read that the Christian is God's workmanship, His poem, as it were (see Eph. 2:10). Since that is how God sees you, that is also how you need to see yourself if you are to have a true view of you.

So then, failure isn't fatal—necessarily. Not if you will look beyond the failure and believe in yourself anyhow, as God does.

"A Task for a Two-Year-Old"

I spent the better part of a day last summer working on my power lawnmower that wouldn't start. I kept getting in deeper and deeper, looking for the trouble, until I had the thing completely dismantled. When I finally got it back together again, it worked exactly as it had when I began—not at all. The frustration, the sense of failure, didn't do much for my attitude, even though the entire project wasn't of earth-shaking importance.

While I'm confessing, I should admit that one of my faults is berating myself for failing to accomplish things as easily and quickly as I would like. Typically, such self-talk goes like this. "I don't believe it! This is a simple task any two-year-old ought to be able to do in five minutes and I suppose I'm going to spend half the day on it."

Of course, I don't believe what I'm saying. Mostly I'm letting off steam. Sometimes, if the product is poorly designed, I will rail against the manufacturer instead of myself. "There's absolutely no excuse for this. Anybody who would design such a monstrosity ought to be shot." Usually, though, I have to battle the feeling that I, in some measure, am at fault.

This is because any failure is likely to bring with it a sense of self-reproach, regardless of the cause. To prove this to yourself you only need to conduct a simple experiment. Break the handle off a cup. Then carefully glue it back on with weak glue that will not hold much weight. Now serve a cup of coffee to some poor unsuspecting guest. Better be sure it's not too hot, however, and that your guest is not wearing fine clothes, because you know what's going to happen. When he picks it up and the handle breaks and coffee spills everywhere, watch what happens.

If the person knows of your trickery he will either be angry at you or amused at the incident. Since he does not know, however, he will likely be full of apologies and act as if he were at fault somehow even though all he did was pick up his cup of coffee.

In other words, just as there is false guilt (see chapter 10), there is also *false failure*. Don't be too quick to assume you failed somehow. You may have been working with a broken cup.

Failure as a Learning Device

If you have ever searched the help wanted columns of the newspaper, you have surely seen the frequent stipulation that applicants be experienced. Employers know that proficiency in almost any job requires certain skills gained only by experience, by practice.

Experience involves failure. That's why the employer demands an experienced worker. He wants one who has already made his mistakes somewhere else and has thus learned to do the work correctly.

Failure, then, is a learning device. And if we

learn from our failures, they are by no means a total loss.

I'm a do-it-yourselfer. I do practically all my own automobile maintenance and repair as well as any fixing that needs done around our place (except lawnmowers!). Recently I completely rebuilt my wife's 1965 Corvair convertible. It was the middle car in a three-car-pile-up (caused by an uninsured motorist), plus it had rusted sills from braving salty winter roads in Illinois where we used to live. I bought another old Corvair for parts and put almost a whole new perimeter on the convertible. I'm quite pleased with the finished product.

I had plenty of "failures" along the way, but I've done enough automotive work to accept that as par for the course, and to persevere. You see, each part I worked with offered the possibility of failure. First I had to remove the part from the old car without damaging it and then I had to install it properly on the car being rebuilt. Every bolt, screw, and clip offered its challenge. If I failed using one tool, I would try another. If a fastener wouldn't yield to my initial effort, I oiled it, heated it, tapped on it, or finally cut it off. Much of the body itself had to be cut off the old car and welded on the new one because that's how it was made in the first place.

Eventually, despite many "failures," I succeeded in rebuilding the car. At the same time, I also increased my skills. Of course, the truth is I was able to tackle such a major job only because for years I had been building my skills, failing again and again but also succeeding, and learning more and more in the process.

That's one reason perseverance is important. If we give up on a task, it is like letting failure be the last word. If we persevere, success becomes the last word, and the incidental failures along the way don't matter. Even the modified success of a task completed less than perfectly is better than the defeat of giving up. It was this truth that Jane Merchant had in mind when she wrote:

Susanna's Apron

"I can plan better things," said Sue,
"Much better things than I can do."
And laughing, so as not to cry,
She ripped out seams that went awry
And sewed them neatly back again
As one can do when one is ten,
And wore the apron with a pride
Considerably dissatisfied,
Saying, "I did the best I could,
But it doesn't look the way it should."

I think that since Susanna's one
Who finishes what she's begun,
Who makes her fair and hopeful plan
And does the very best she can,
She'll surely someday find her seams
Entirely equal to her dreams.[2]

So far we have said that failure isn't fatal if you will

- Believe in yourself as God believes in you
- Reject false failure—when it's not your fault
- Learn from your failures—increase your skills.

And now we are saying:

Don't Let Failure Have the Last Word

One good thing about failure is that it is temporary. One may fail at something many times but wipe out the negative effect completely by later succeeding.

Last year we sold a house. We did it ourselves without the aid of a realtor. The first people who phoned in response to our "For Sale" sign did not buy the place. In fact, they didn't even show up at the appointed time to inspect it. The first time we advertised it in the newspaper it didn't sell either. Nor the second time. Nor the third.

We might have given up. We might have accepted failure and turned the house over to professionals, but we'd been this route before. We knew they had no magic, and that in the seller's market existing at the time we could sell the place if the price was right.

And so we did. We had to turn down a number of unsatisfactory offers. Several prospective buyers disappointed us by deciding against the purchase. But after about two months the right people came along with the right offer, and we had a sale.

All the failures meant nothing. Do you suppose we are one bit bothered now by the many individual experiences of not selling our house? Of course not. We look back on the single experience of success. The bottom line was *we did it*.

My wife commented, "People give up too easily. They put their place up for sale by owner and if nobody grabs it in the first week or two they list it with a realtor. Then they give the professional three months to do the same job they allowed themselves only a few days to do. If they'd be as patient with themselves as they are with the realtor they probably would not need him."

I'm not saying one should not use the services of a realtor. Under certain circumstances I would use one myself. What I'm saying is that failure is often a prelude to achievement. I'm also saying that since failure is psychologically degrading, one needs to persist beyond failure to success if at all possible.

Jane Merchant, of whom we spoke earlier, was severely handicapped, but she had a strong desire to be a useful and productive person. Naturally, she experienced her share of failures. Out of such experiences she wrote the following poem describing perfectly the attitude we need to adopt when we've failed:

After Failure

The careful, unremitting work
I did has not availed.
I gave my best to one large task,
And now I know I failed.

Today I'll do the little things,
The things I can do best.
I'll do the little easy things
And give my heart a rest.

A dozen little things, well done,
Will lighten failure's sorrow
And give me strength to try, once more,
A larger task tomorrow.[3]

We may be sure that those we think of as successful reached that goal via many failures.

Do you imagine that all the works of Shakespeare were literary gems? Nobody knows what tripe he may have written in his early days. And nobody cares. Any early failures are forgotten because he later succeeded.

Lincoln's failures are almost classic. At age 22

he found himself unemployed because the store where he worked went broke. He soon ran for the Illinois legislature, but lost. At age 24, he went into business with a man named Berry, buying three small stores. The business failed and Lincoln was stuck with a debt that took him 15 years to pay.

When Lincoln was 26 his sweetheart died. The next year he suffered a nervous breakdown. When he was 39 the people of Illinois rejected him after he had served only one term in the House of Representatives. Ten years later he was up for nomination for the vice-presidency of the country but failed to get enough support. At age 49, Lincoln ran for the United States Senate and lost; it was his second failing attempt at that office. Two years later, Lincoln became president. Today he is remembered as one of America's greatest leaders; the failures are all forgotten.

One of the greatest geniuses of modern times was Albert Einstein. Yet, as a child, he was so quiet and withdrawn that some thought him retarded. When his parents asked his headmaster what career their son might best follow, he replied, "It doesn't matter; he'll never make a success of anything."

As a young man, Einstein was unable to get a teaching position, for which he had prepared, and had to settle for clerk in the Swiss patent office, a job he stayed in for many years.

When some of his revolutionary scientific theories were confirmed, Einstein vaulted to world prominence, and in 1921 he received the Nobel prize. His genius had simply gone unrecognized before.

But even a genius makes mistakes and fails in

his efforts. Einstein once said, "I think and think, for months, for years; 99 times the conclusion is false. The hundredth time I am right."

According to that statement, the difference between success and failure for Albert Einstein was the difference between accepting failure as the final word after 99 times versus persevering always one more time.

That does not mean Einstein was the dogged never-give-up type who kept repeating the same mistakes. No, we may safely assume he learned from each failure. Each time he was wrong he was that much closer to being right. He had eliminated one error and taken one step closer to discovery of the truth. In that sense, no failure was a total failure. Every failure was useful. And every failure was only a temporary pause on the way to success.

This brings us to one last principle for coping with failure:

Set Multiple Realistic Goals

Failure or success is a somewhat subjective thing. No one can appropriately attach either label to your endeavors unless they know what your goals are. Ordinarily, you are the one who should decide that.

Suppose I were to enter the 26-mile Boston Marathon. You are an acquaintance of mine and you are waiting at the finish line to see how I do. At last the front runners come into view and I am not among them. *Too bad*, you think, *the poor guy not only won't win but he isn't even among the top ten contenders. What a failure*!

About an hour later, I come staggering across the finish line. You are groping for something to say to console me, but then you notice I don't need consoling. I am extremely pleased with my performance. It turns out that I didn't enter to win. My goal was to finish, and I have succeeded.

I might have set a number of other "lesser" goals as well. Simply to make the trip to Boston and enter the marathon could have been my goal. By my example to encourage a hesitant friend of mine with far more potential than me to take up long-distance running could have been my goal.

Now, if I accomplish what I set out to do, can that be considered a failure? That's what I'd call a success.

Thomas Edison is said to have conducted some 18,000 experiments in developing the electric light bulb. Does that mean he failed 17,999 times? Not at all. When he tried a platinum filament and it quickly burned out, he had succeeded in eliminating that design. His other experiments similarly succeeded in eliminating other possibilities. His ultimate goal was an electric light bulb, but his intermediate goals were many.

The time to think about your goals is before you begin. There may be occasions when you will decide that you should undertake some endeavor the "success" of which is unlikely. You may want to enter some race you have little realistic hope of winning. OK, be clear about that at the beginning. Identify the things you do hope to accomplish. Then your heart will not call failure what was really a noble success.

The daily "failures" that are a part of everyone's experience need not destroy you, or even damage you, if you apply the principles set forth in this chapter. What were they, in summary?

Believe in yourself despite failings—as God does.

Reject false failure—when you're not at fault.

Learn from your failures—increase your skills.

Don't let failure have the last word—go on to success.

Set multiple realistic goals so that, though you fail at some, you will achieve others at the same time.

Notes

1. Craig Selness, *From Frustration to Fulfillment*, (Wheaton: SP Publications, Inc.), 1982.
2. Jane Merchant, "Susanna's Apron," *Think About These Things* (Nashville: Abingdon Press, 1956), Copyright © 1956 by Pierce and Washabaugh. Used by permission.
3. Jane Merchant, "After Failure," *In Green Pastures* Copyright © 1959 by Abingdon Press. Used by permission.

Chapter 12

Disaster: Failing Big

Some failures are not easily absorbed. The principles of the previous chapter, however helpful in ordinary circumstances, may offer slight comfort to a person caught in major, traumatic failure. Such a person might understandably cry, "Don't talk to me about little piddly failures; I've got a disaster on my hands."

Dale Galloway endured such an experience. He writes:

> On a cloudy day in the fall of 1969, I was sitting in a restaurant on Southeast 82nd Street in Portland, Oregon, unaware of the catastrophe about to strike my life. Seated across the table from me was the girl I had fallen in love with as a freshman in college. We had married in the summer of 1957 and had struggled together to get me through college, seminary, and the beginning years of my pastoral ministry. Now the struggle

> for economic survival was over. At age 30, I was enjoying the success of pastoring one of the larger churches of our denomination in the state of Oregon. The future had never looked brighter.
>
> Then it happened. The volcano of pent-up emotions erupted. My wife of twelve years angrily pointed her finger at me and said, "I do not love you. I never have loved you, and I'm going to divorce you." The sentence of death had been pronounced.
>
> Nothing worse could have happened to me as a minister brought up in a God-fearing, Bible-believing, conservative church and home. The collapse of my marriage meant that in the eyes of my church family I was a failure. A failure as a husband, a failure as a minister, and even a failure as a Christian. At this time I experienced the emptiness of feeling rejected, unloved. Is there any more devastating feeling?[1]

Dale described just how devastating this experience and its aftermath were in his first book: *Dream a New Dream*.

> Having lost all sense of time, I wandered aimlessly along an unknown beach in the State of Washington. I was sobbing uncontrollably every step of the way. As the sun was going down and darkness was closing in, I dropped down on the beach completely exhausted. For me the sun had stopped shining; there was only darkness.
>
> "Where the hell are you, God?" I

shouted. Just a few brief months before, I would not have believed any true minister of God would think such words, let alone shout them angrily again and again at the top of his voice. . . . Before ending up on that beach, at the bottom emotionally, I had gone four days without food, fasting and praying, calling on God to, by some miracle, save our marriage. Now, as I lay on the beach, I knew the marriage was over. My life as a minister would soon be wrecked. My children would be taken many miles away from me. Never before had we had a divorce in my immediate family and I didn't see how any of the family could ever accept me again.

My father, whom I loved and for whom I had great respect, had not only been a minister for as long as I could remember, but had for the past thirty years been the head administrator of our denomination in the State of Ohio. My dad's brother had also been a prominent minister. Both my grandfathers had helped to pioneer, and had literally sacrificed everything they had to help establish, the denomination that our family now enjoyed so very much. I grew up knowing how the church thought almost as well as I knew my own thoughts. Instinctively, I knew that there was no way that the people from this conservative, evangelical background would ever be able to understand my divorce. I would forever be, in their eyes, a "second-class citizen." In my

> brokenness and out of the anguish of my soul I cried, "Where the hell are you, God? Don't you care? Haven't I served you since I was fifteen years old? Haven't I tried to do everything that you have wanted me to do? I have never said 'no' to anything you wanted in my life. Where are you now? Don't you even care that I'm going down for the last time?"[2]

Today Dale Galloway is pastor of the thriving New Hope Community Church in Portland, Oregon, a ministry dedicated to "healing hurts and building dreams." Through the church's varied ministries, through his writing, and through his television programs, Dale has helped many other devastated people rise to their feet and walk with God as never before.

How did Dale come back from such abject and crushing failure? From failure so great that he virtually felt he was under sentence of death? He writes:

> For the first time my will to die was stronger than my will to live because everything that I lived for I was losing.
>
> Do you know what saved my life? Do you know what kept me going when I didn't feel like getting out of bed in the morning? What gave me hope when people around me said I was a wash-out? I got into the heart of the Bible and encountered Jesus in a new fresh way.
>
> I saw Him suffer and die on a cross for my sins. He died for my failings, my shortcomings, my mistakes, my sins, and whatever else anybody wants to call it. The truth is that whatever is wrong

with me and whatever is wrong with you, He died on that cross to forgive it and make it right.[3]

God Is Bigger than You Think

No matter how many times you have failed in the past, no matter how desperately you have failed, with God there is hope. Not just a glimmer of hope, but a bright and shining hope.

Christians have sometimes been known to wail and cry about having "missed the will of God," as if some fateful failure of the past now dooms them to failure forever. That's mostly nonsense. We've all missed the will of God because we have all sinned. God is neither unforgiving nor unresourceful, and He can overrule our failures.

Nobody ever failed more as an individual than Israel did as a nation. Because of Israel's sin and failure ancient prophets not only pronounced judgment of God on the nation but also despaired sometimes of any hope for her future. About the judgment for sin, they were right. About no hope for the future, they were wrong, and God told them so.

God sent one of His prophets, Jeremiah, down to the house of the potter to learn this lesson. There Jeremiah saw a significant thing. "The pot he was shaping from the clay was marred in his hands; so the potter formed it into another pot, shaping it as seemed best to him" (Jer. 18:4).

God is not so lacking in creativity that He cannot think of anything worthwhile to do with a lump of human clay that has shown some defects as He has worked with it. He is quite able to fashion another vessel that seems good to Him. *Good* to Him. Not just passable, but good in the eyes of God.

The same passage in Jeremiah goes on to suggest how mischievous is the attitude: "I've failed so what's the use?" That's too convenient an excuse for continuing in failure and sin. They said, "It's no use. We will continue with our own plans; each of us will follow the stubbornness of his evil heart" (v. 12).

Do you know what Jeremiah did as an expression of hope in the midst of failure so great that it demanded the people of Israel lose their land and be carried away captives? He bought property.

Get the picture now! Jeremiah was under house arrest. The whole country was going down the drain. Enemy armies surrounded the city of Jerusalem, and Jeremiah was in big trouble with the king for prophesying a total enemy victory. The nation was on the brink of destruction.

About this time, Jeremiah's cousin showed up and offered to sell him a field. I don't know if he thought Jeremiah was the world's biggest sucker or what, but Jeremiah made the purchase. "For this is what the Lord Almighty, the God of Israel, says; 'Houses, fields and vineyards will again be bought in this land' " (Jer. 32:15).

Jeremiah is often called the weeping prophet, but he was also a prophet of hope. Which brings us to another consideration.

Can We Ever Really Start Over?

What has happened in the past cannot be changed. It can be forgiven but it cannot be undone. In that sense, no brand new beginning is possible. Nor would it be desirable if it were possible.

> We are exhorted and indeed come to believe that we can and should make "fresh starts," to "begin all over again,"

> and "to do it better next time around." We must accept mistakes, impurities, and blows to pride positions as a natural part of our lives so we don't always need fresh starts and *can* feel better without having to "do it all over again." This usually is an illusionary desire to do it *perfectly* this time around, without any trace of human mistakes. Interestingly, people suffering from schizophrenia sometimes attempt suicide, feeling that in dying a rebirth will be possible, in which they can begin all over again unsullied by past impurities. Of course this is the height of self-hate. If we accept the human condition, and this includes the many human mistakes and indiscretions that exist, we lose the desire to wipe the slate clean and to be reborn. In accepting our human fallibilities we see life as a continuum of all kinds of experiences and we refuse to surrender any segment of that continuum. If we could and did begin again each time we erred in any way, we would kill all possiblility of experiential wisdom. We would remain pure, unsullied, bland—*and blank.*[4]

Not only should we gain wisdom from our failures of the past, but also we should gain a great deal of compassion for others. Dale Galloway comments:

> I have never seen a man or woman yet who was able to live well with success who had not first traveled through the fires and storms of failure. It is failure

> that keeps a man remembering, when he is successful, how other people hurt and feel.[5]

No, you can't start all over, not in the absolute sense. But you can go on from here to be a better person, more compassionate toward others, and more useful in the hands of God than you ever would have been without experiencing that failure which seems—and is—so terrible now.

It's OK to Cry Over Spilt Milk

We have tried in these chapters to take a positive but realistic view of failure. We have seen many reasons to take courage and be hopeful, no matter what our failures have been.

Nothing we have said, however, implies that it is wrong to feel bad about failing. That's nonsense. Should I make you feel bad because you feel bad when you fail? Should I add to your load by saying you are now failing to handle failure?

In a profound way, Jesus is our supreme example of how to deal with failure. That may seem shocking to say, for Jesus was perfect, wasn't He? He never failed, did He?

It's true that Jesus never was at fault. However, He certainly lived through experiences that would be perceived as failure by most people. And He knew what it felt like to be rejected.

Jesus failed to win the faith and allegiance of the people of Israel. He wept over the city of Jerusalem because of that, saying, "If you . . . had only known on this day what would bring you peace—but now it is hidden from your eyes" (Luke 19:42).

We may tell people not to indulge in "if onlys," but Jesus did. We may say not to feel bad over failures, but Jesus did. Granted, He felt bad for the people, not for Himself. He wept because of their tragic loss. Nevertheless, He was not the cool, detached, calculating type who declares that everything will come out well in the end so let's not be concerned.

Unwavering faith in God rules out despair but it does not exempt us from sorrow. So it's all right to cry over spilt milk. It's OK to hate it when you fail. What is not OK is to hate yourself, to keep feeling guilty when you've been forgiven, to cry so long and hard over spilt milk that you're unable to clean up the mess and go on.

You see, it's the finish that counts, and you are not finished yet. Not unless you are dead.

> It was the night before the intercollegiate games. I was a freshman at Yale. The Captain stood under my room on the fifth floor of old North and called up to me that I was to run the mile the next day at Berkeley Oval in New York. That shout in the dark gave me one of the greatest thrills of my life.
>
> Two o'clock the following afternoon found me in the Yale training quarters at the Oval. The Captain, ostentatiously cool and collected, told me that Yale, the Freshman Class, and nearly all right-minded, civilized people were anxious to have me win the Mile that day. I was entirely willing to oblige them.
>
> Then old Mike Murphy, the best trainer the world has ever known, muttered some advice in my ear about not getting pocketed and laying back until the last quarter. Sid, the rubber, slapped

raw alcohol on my bare back, gave my legs a farewell rub, and someone shouted through the door: "Last call for the Mile."

The next moment I was out upon the track, which was ringed around with stands full of shouting, cheering spectators. Thirty or forty of us contestants got on our marks in three lines that stretched clear across the cinder path.

"Get set," the starter shouted. Then came the bang of a pistol—and we were off.

One of the boys who ran that day was an almost unknown runner, representing a small school. At the first corner, while fighting for the lead, he was accidentally spiked and thrown headlong. One of his legs was gashed by the long spikes on the shoes of another competitor, and his hands and face were cut by the cinders. By the time he had struggled to his feet, the whole field was thirty yards ahead.

He had fallen. His face was blackened and bleeding; he was left far behind. It seemed hopeless for him to go on; nevertheless he started after the crowd of runners as bravely as if nothing had happened.

All around the first lap he remained behind them all. Little by little, however, he began to cut down the lead of runners nearest him, and by the end of the first half he was up among the laggards of the race, twenty yards back of the leaders.

Then came that bitter third quarter.

Nothing is harder in athletics than the third quarter of a fast mile. One has already run a half at full speed, and there is still another quarter to come. An iron band seems to tighten around one's chest. There is the salt taste of blood in the mouth, and one longs to give up, and fall down and rest.

Yet that boy, who had been last, blackened and bleeding, with set teeth, cut down one faltering runner after another of those farthest behind, until, as the leaders neared the finish of the third lap, they heard behind them the pad, pad of flying feet coming nearer and nearer.

In another moment the pacemakers had reached the fourth quarter, and a deep-toned bell signalled the beginning of the last lap, while the cheers of the crowd swept across the track like a storm.

The sound was like a spur to the speed of that boy who had been last. He shot by a little group of runners, and in the backstretch was hard upon the heels of the four leaders. As they swung around the last corner into the homestretch, those four who were in front heard the sound of flying feet approaching them from behind, and knew that the race that day was to be fought out by five instead of four.

As all five of them swung into the homestretch, the spectators leaned forward from the stands and called upon the runners by name for one last desperate effort. No one called on the boy who ran last of that quintette, nor even knew his name.

At the finish a strand of red worsted was stretched breast-high across the track. The runner who first broke that cord was the mile champion for the coming year. There were grouped the judges and the timers; and to the men struggling toward it, that red line seemed to move back to an interminable distance.

The extreme limit of their endurance had been reached, and as their strength flagged, each runner called upon the very soul that was in him to help him bear the pain and carry him on to the finish. Lurching and staggering with mortal weakness, each one drew upon the last atom of strength in him for the final effort.

A strange silence fell upon the crowd, and in the stillness the rapid, laboured breathing of the runners could be heard. Suddenly, level with the fourth man, came the blackened, gashed face of the last runner, and slowly drew away from him.

Now the finish was only thirty yards away, and suddenly beside the third man showed that same disfigured face, whose staring eyes saw nothing but the goal. That third man did his best and gave all he had to hold his place—I ought to know, I was that third man—but slowly and surely the boy who had fallen at the

> start drew away from him.
>
> Then he challenged the other two, who were running neck and neck, and five yards from the finish drew even with them. For an instant that seemed a year the three struggled for the lead, and then, at the very finish, the runner who had been left lying prostrate in the dirt when the race began, threw himself forward, broke the tape a scant inch ahead of the other two, won the race, and broke the Intercollegiate Record for the Mile.
>
> In forty years of athletics I have never seen again so gallant a finish, and to the day of my death will never forget that race nor that runner.
>
> In the lives of all of us there are times when we stumble and fall and are defiled by the dirt, and cut and gashed and hurt. Yet we are beaten only if we give up and lie down hopeless and helpless. No matter how far the fall or how dreadful the failure, there is only one thing to do—get up and go on and on and never, never quit! The start is important, but—it's the finish that wins![6]

You and I are in a different situation from the runner in the foregoing true story. After all, that was only a race. The fallen runner could have simply walked from the track and likely would have received more sympathy than blame. Neither does his beating out his opponents have any relevance to us. We don't have to excel anyone else.

But what the runner did in that race, we must do in life. We must not just lie there when we fall. We must not give up and walk off the track. We can yet win. I don't mean win over others—that doesn't matter. But we can win over despair and self-reproach. We can win where it counts.

Notes

1. Dale E. Galloway, *Something More Than a Dream.* © 1981 by Dale E. Galloway. Used by permission.
2. Dale E. Galloway, *Rebuild Your Life* (formerly *Dream a New Dream*; Wheaton, IL: Tyndale House Publishers, 1975) © Copyright by Dale E. Galloway. Used by permission.
3. Galloway, *Something More Than a Dream.*
4. Theodore Isaac Rubin, *Compassion and Self-Hate* (New York: David McKay Company, 1975), pp. 294,295.
5. Galloway, *Something More Than a Dream.*
6. Samuel Scoville, Jr., "The Last Lap," *Sunday School Times.*

Chapter 13

Alienation: Failing in Our Relationships

Is there anything that can tear us up more than being trapped in a hurting or broken relationship? For most people the answer is all too painfully clear. No, nothing is harder, nothing is worse.

John Powell writes:

> Only recently have the behavioral sciences reached the point of enlightenment to show us that unconditional love is the only soil in which the seed of a human person can grow.
>
> Of course, free will is a factor in every human life. Everyone must say his or her "yes" to growth and integrity. But there are prerequisites. And one of these is that someone must empower me to believe in myself and to be myself. Only someone who loves me unconditionally can do this.[1]

Strong claims, those. Unconditional love is *the*

only soil in which human personality can grow? If that's true, it's no wonder we feel like uprooted plants, dying on the vine, when our relationships are wrong.

Powell also writes, in the same book:

> The most perceptive insight of contemporary personalism is that I become a person only if I receive my personhood from someone else through the gift of affirmation. If I never see myself valued by others, I will never value myself. To this the psychiatrist Viktor Frankl enjoins this absolutely necessary advice: True self-esteem and a true sense of identity can be found only in the reflected appraisal of those whom we have loved.[2]

In what could seem to be a conflicting vein, we have said that a self-image based on feedback from other people, while very common, is likely to be faulty. Our theme has been that a correct self-concept must come from God instead of from "the world."

It may be true that "I become a person only if I receive my personhood from someone else through the gift of affirmation." However, that "someone else" may be, should be, and for some deprived people *must* be God. Otherwise, if the important people in our lives disavow our worth, we are hopeless, doomed to a life of self-reproach and nonpersonhood.

There is no question but that affirmation from those closest to us helps, but if we say it's essential we offer no hope to those who simply don't get such affirmation but, to the contrary, are continually degraded.

I believe there is hope. The experience of Robby

and his sister, told in chapter 8, constitutes evidence that God can get through to people personally and directly with the assurance that He loves them. It may take a crisis, and the message from God may want reinforcement from loving people later. Still, God does touch people who feel worthless. He does let downcast people know that, to Him, they are of great value.

Sharon Johnson had such an experience. Because God Himself got through to her when she had no one else, she was rescued from self-reproachful suicide. She writes:

> My head throbbed and nausea swept over me. I was nearly unconscious at last, my knees weak and trembling as I stood near the exhaust of my car in our closed garage.
>
> *Why is it taking so long*? I wondered. The stench of exhaust fumes filled my head and I detested the sick feeling in my stomach. I hadn't read about that, and for a moment I felt angry that this information had been denied me.
>
> The traumas of the past few months flashed before me. My husband's affair with another woman, the sordid details haunting me constantly; his rejection of me in favor of her; my children's accusations against me in their painful separation from their dad, who had misled them about the reasons for his departure.
>
> In the end, I'd simply had no strength left. My husband was right, I told myself. I had failed to make him happy. I had failed my children. They would be much

better off in the care of someone else. The physical beatings my husband had given me—I supposed I'd deserved those too.

My mind had been foggy for days now. Half-empty coffee cups, poured and forgotten, sat in various places throughout the house. Dirty dishes filled the sink at the end of the day. *Had I fed the children or were they yesterday's dishes?* I couldn't remember.

Why had God given my children to me, a failure? I would remember to ask Him that. All I wanted at this moment was to be with Jesus, to feel His arms around me.

Suddenly a movement jarred my thoughts back to the present. I realized my knees had buckled and I reached out to the car for support. Knowing time was short, I attempted to form a mental picture of God welcoming me into heaven. Something wasn't right. I felt like a child being scolded.

"Do you really want to face Me this way?" a voice spoke softly into my mind. Reality hit me like a bullet. *God loves me! He wants me alive. Obedience will bring me into eternity in His timing, not mine.*

I reached for the garage door. My body responded slowly. My hand felt like jelly as it hit the door and moved downward to the handle. I gripped it and pulled, but it wouldn't move. *Locked*!

The smoke-filled air burned my eyes and I couldn't see. Was I to die here, my choice to take my life being confirmed even though I had changed my mind? In panic I prayed, "Lord, forgive me!"

The latch snapped open in my hand, and when I yanked, the door went up quickly. Bright sunlight mixed with the polluted air as I tried to adjust my vision to the surroundings. There was my neighbor's house across the street. The sky was blue and clear and the yard fresh and green. The rhododendron bush was in bloom, its pink and purple blossoms gently nodding in the breeze.

The faces of my three beautiful daughters flashed to mind. *God had trusted me as their mother, husband or not.* I could raise them with His help.

That simple affirmation was the beginning of a new self-image and a new life for me. My progress has been slow at times and the lessons many since that day nine years ago. Sometimes I take one step forward and two back, but less and less frequently. Verses such as 1 John 4:4 help: "Greater is He that is in you than he that is in the world." God is in me, and that, not some other person's approval, makes me worthwhile. Never again will I allow another human being to control my sense of worth.

Looking back I ask why I ever allowed myself to dwell on my failures. Then I realize that my mistake was in making my husband lord of my life. My self-esteem for eleven years was dependent on him. His acceptance and approval gov-

> erned my opinion of myself completely, until my eyes were opened to this error.
>
> Today my heart aches for those in bondage in situations similar to mine. Wives cringe as I did when orders are yelled at them by unloving husbands. With their confidence crushed by harsh words and name-calling, they feel worthless, condemned both by others and by themselves. How I pray that God's love and acceptance will get through to them!
>
> To the rejected, I would say: remember, the perfect Jesus was condemned and rejected too. Yet God said, "This is My beloved Son, in whom I am well pleased." If we have trusted in Jesus Christ, we are a 10 in God's eyes though we fail daily, for He sees the final product—His image perfectly reflected in us.[3]

These days more and more marriages fail. We're often told there is really no "innocent party" in such cases. Both partners have contributed to the breakdown of marriage. Perhaps so, but that very attitude is a put-down and can complicate the self-esteem problem for the divorced person. He or she gets the message: *you have failed, permanently*. Never mind if your mate was hooked on drugs or alcohol, abused you physically and verbally, or turned out to be a homosexual both in tendency and practice.

The teaching of some Christians aggravates the problem by stating or implying that it takes only one partner to make a marriage work. Women especially are led to believe that if they are submissive enough and spiritual enough their husbands will be transformed. This claim is usually supported with glowing success stories of women who did it. The teaching serves only to beat down those who find it doesn't work that way for them—even though they try it, perhaps for years.

Put-downs and failure get all mixed together in situations like this. We don't know how much of our bad feeling about ourselves comes from others' attitudes and how much from our own sense of failure. Either way, our self-esteem is devastated.

Other Types of Rejection

A troubled relationship can damage us even if it is not such an important and intimate one as marriage. Any time we sense rejection from another person, we tend to feel failure, because we want people to like us. We want them to think well of us. More important, we want to think well of ourselves, and when someone else shows he does not think well of us we are afraid he might be right.

This is what wipes out many sales people. They can't take the rejection. They tell themselves that the prospect's refusal to purchase is no reflection on them, but they have a hard time believing it.

I asked my friend Tom Mullins, a trainer of sales people, how much rejection a person can take. "The average person can't take any," he said, to my surprise. "Reject him once and it's all over. He crashes in flames."

We all know people whose lives seem to contradict that evaluation—children who keep bidding for affirmation and attention from unresponsive parents, wives who keep talking at husbands who aren't listening, and husbands who keep trying to buy their wives' affections. But in these cases, the rejected person is also a trapped and desperate person with little choice but to keep trying.

When a close relationship already exists, people swallow rejection and persevere in the relationship partly because, as we've said, failing in relationships is so painful and threatening. But by the same token, people ordinarily steer clear of new relationships that seem headed for difficulty. At the first hint of rejection from someone we're not already tied to, we turn away.

Many times, if a neighbor snubs us once, that's it. He won't get a second chance. We don't need any more rejection that will only make us feel bad about ourselves. As a result of initial failure in reaching out to people, then, we often withdraw. To the degree such withdrawal becomes typical of us, it isolates us from other people. However, this is detrimental to our self-esteem almost as much as rejection would be. We soon come to see ourselves as not adept at making friends and therefore not likable.

Withdrawing is detrimental to our personal growth also, for it is often in relating to others that we grow the most. But what if you are caught in your isolation? What if you are a loner? What can you do about it?

John Powell suggests that each of us needs one close friend with whom we can relate freely and honestly. Such a friend-confidant must be one who will "give us full freedom to have and express our feelings." Powell continues:

> Alfred Adler says that a warm human relationship is necessary to give people the courage needed to face and understand their mistakes. Knowing that someone loves us unconditionally enables us to face and admit our delu-

sions. This is also one of the main principles of Carl Rogers in his theory of counseling. We can understand and accept ourselves realistically only when someone outside ourselves first understands and accepts us. Consequently, Adler and others recommend that, if a person does not have and cannot make such a friend, he or she might have to join some kind of a warm and receptive group.

Dialogue and discussion with such a friend-confidant make still another very definite contribution in helping us to locate our misconceptions. We have to organize a problem before we can talk it over with another. Very often, if left to ourselves, we do not go through this organization of the problem and its ramifications. Our problems remain vague and diffuse when kept inside us. With a friend-confidant we must not only organize but we must also verbalize the problem. This reality of verbalization is extremely important. The way we verbalize a situation often determines how we will evaluate it. Very often our reactions are determined by the words we choose to describe the situation. We think in words, plan our lives with words, and tend to be very much defined by our own verbalizations. This is why some have recommended repeating at regular daily intervals positive words or mottoes such as "I am! I can! I will!" If we are interpreting and verbalizing a given situation in a lopsided manner, dialogue with a friend will tend to help us back to balance and objectivity.[4]

This kind of relationship is extremely helpful if not essential to personal growth. It must be based, however, on honest, open, and egalitarian attitudes. Too often, other dynamics prevent the development of this kind of relationship. Just getting two or more people together won't do it. As Paul wrote to the Corinthians, their get-togethers, even at their love feasts, were more damaging than helpful (see 1 Cor. 11:17).

What keeps our relationships from becoming the mutual benefit and blessing that we all need them to be?

Playing Top Dog

Bob has an intimidating style of relating to others that has developed over long years. Actually, it is a neurotic device to bolster his self-esteem, though Bob doesn't have the remotest clue to that fact.

His behavior consists of immediately seeking to establish himself in a superior position each time you meet him. He has numerous techniques for doing this—all refined to an art.

His favorite tactic is to make a comment or ask a question that puts you on the defensive. He does this good-naturedly, but that's just to mask the purpose of it.

Bob says things like, "Hey, I didn't see you in church last Sunday." If someone else said that to you, it might be a wholesome expression of interest, a way of letting you know you were missed. With Bob, the purpose is something else altogether. You are now supposed to explain to him why you were not in church. The reasons you offer don't matter. The point is that you are in a position of answering to him for your actions, as if you were some sort of underling.

Or Bob may greet you with, "Where's your wife? Left her home again, huh?" Once more, what you say by way of explanation doesn't matter. Now you're accounting to him for your personal home life.

Looking at his watch as you arrive, Bob may say, "I expected you a little earlier." He will follow that up with some specious reason the exact time of your arrival matters. If you are even one minute late you are now supposed to be duly apologetic. If you are actually on time you are supposed to feel like you should have been early. Either way, you are to defer to the top dog.

Had you come earlier, however, you may be sure Bob would have said something intimidating about that, for it's not what you do that is the problem; it's Bob's need to play top dog.

If you know someone who constantly makes you feel inferior or on trial, try to detach yourself enough to observe the interaction between the two of you. You may well find someone is playing top dog with you.

What can you do about it? Several things.

First, just recognizing what's happening—and why and how—can help you put things in perspective. Realizing that the other person has an emotional malfunction and that it's really his problem more than yours takes a lot of the pain out of the situation.

Second, if you can't handle his continual intimidation you may want to limit the relationship.

Third, you can challenge the behavior. To come

right out and accuse a person of playing top dog may alienate him, but the relationship is already dismal so you don't have a lot to lose. However, a better way might be simply to stop playing his game. When he comes at you with his top-dog tactics, you don't lie down and roll over.

You might say, "Let's not begin our visit by me explaining or defending myself. It makes me feel as if you are finding fault with me. That's not your intention, is it?"

One or two encounters like that and top dog will probably change his treatment of you—let up a little. He might even pause to reflect on what his habitual behavior says about him.

Being a Victim

Another negative way of relating is as a victim. Dr. Wayne Dyer has written of this at length, and the following passage is to the point:

> Think back to the very first time your spouse abused you, by raising his voice, getting angry, hitting you, or whatever. . . .
>
> Suppose that instead of being shocked, stunned, afraid or tearful, you had showed your partner your hand, told him that it was a registered weapon, and given him a solid karate chop to the stomach, followed up with, "I don't intend to take that kind of abuse from you. I think of myself as a person with dignity, and I'm not ever going to be shoved around by you or anyone else. Please give yourself a heavy dose of second thoughts before you try something

like that again. That's all I have to say about it." And then you proceeded to carry on an intelligent conversation.

While this may seem an absurd thing to imagine, it illustrates the point: Had you reacted from strength and firm intolerance for abusive behavior right from the very beginning, you would once and for all have taught your partner something very important—that you will not indulge such nasty behavior for one second.

But your reaction was probably disastrously different. Whether you cried, acted hurt or insulted, or showed fear, you sent out a fatal signal that you would not necessarily like the way he was treating you, but that you would take it, and even more significantly, that you would let yourself be manipulated emotionally by it.

When I told Gayle this theory she said, "I could never have reacted anything like the way you say I might have!" At first she wanted to defend her entrenched position that her husband and her children were totally at fault for her victim status, and she wanted me to feel sorry for her and become an ally in her misery. When I persisted in stating that the "karate chop" doesn't need violence, physical or any other kind, to have its psychological impact, and that she might have left the room, refused to talk with him, or even called the police, to illustrate her intolerance, she began to get the message. She

> soon accepted the fact that she had indeed taught almost everyone that she was willing to be a "dumpee," and she resolved to work at changing from then on.[5]

Some may feel it's "not Christian" to stand up for one's dignity as Dyer suggests. To the contrary, failing to do so is what's not Christian because it is inconsistent with love. No one should be either a victim or a victimizer. If you are a victim, and you allow such a sinful relationship to continue, you are doing a decided disservice to everyone involved.

As a Cardboard Character

A third counter-productive way of relating is superficially. It is refusing to open up and be real with others in our lives. When this happens, people deal with one another as cardboard characters instead of flesh and blood human beings.

John Powell gives an example of the dramatic change for the better that can come about when superficiality yields to openness.

> Some twelve years ago, I stood watching my university students file into the classroom for our first session in the Theology of Faith. That was the day I first saw Tommy. My eyes and my mind both blinked. He was combing his long flaxen hair, which hung six inches below his shoulders, it was the first time I had ever seen a boy with hair that long. I guess it was just coming into fashion then. I know in my mind that it isn't what's on your head but in it that counts; but on that day I was unprepared and my emo-

tions flipped. I immediately filed Tommy under "S" for strange . . . very strange.

Tommy turned out to be the "atheist in residence" in my Theology of Faith course. He constantly objected to, smirked at, or whined about the possibility of an unconditionally loving Father-God. We lived with each other in relative peace for one semester, although I admit he was for me at times a serious pain in the back pew. When he came up at the end of the course to turn in his final exam, he asked in a slightly cynical tone: "Do you think I'll ever find God?" I decided instantly on a little shock therapy. "No!" I said very emphatically. "Oh," he responded, "I thought that was the product you were pushing." I let him get five steps from the classroom door and then called out: "Tommy! I don't think you'll ever find him, but I am absolutely certain that he will find you!" He shrugged a little and left my class and my life (temporarily). I felt slightly disappointed at the thought that he had missed my clever line: "He will find you!" At least I thought it was clever.

Later I heard that Tom was graduated and I was duly grateful. Then a sad report. I heard that Tommy had terminal cancer. Before I could search him out, he came to see me. When he walked into my office, his body was very badly wasted, and the long hair had all fallen out as a result of chemotherapy. But his eyes were bright and his voice was firm, for the first time, I think. "Tommy, I've thought about you so often. I hear you are sick!" I blurted out.

"Oh, yes, very sick. I have cancer in both lungs. It's a matter of weeks."

"Can you talk about it, Tom?"

"Sure, what would you like to know?"

"What's it like to be only twenty-four and dying?"

"Well, it could be worse."

"Like what?"

"Well, like being fifty and having no values or ideals, like being fifty and thinking that booze, seducing women, and making money are the real 'biggies' in life."

I began to look through my mental file cabinet under "S" where I had filed Tom as strange. (I swear that everybody I try to reject by classification God sends back into my life to educate me.)

"But what I really came to see you about," Tom said, "is something you said to me on the last day of class." (He remembered!)

He continued, "I asked you if you thought I would ever find God and you said, 'No!' which surprised me. Then you said, 'But he will find you.' I thought about that a lot, even though my search for God was hardly intense at that time. (My "clever" line. He thought about that a lot!)

"But when the doctors removed a lump from my groin and told me that it was malignant, then I got serious about locating God. And when the malignancy spread into my vital organs, I really began banging bloody fists against the bronze doors of heaven. But God did not come out. In fact, nothing happened. Did you ever try anything for a long time with great effort and with no success? You get psychologically glutted, fed up with trying. And then you quit. Well, one day I woke up, and instead of throwing a few more futile appeals over that high brick wall to a God who may be or may not be there, I just quit. I decided that I didn't really care . . . about God, about an after-life, or anything like that.

"I decided to spend what time I had left doing something more profitable. I thought about you and your class and I remembered something else you had said: 'The essential sadness is to go through life without loving. But it would be almost equally sad to go through life and leave this world without ever telling those you loved that you had loved them.'

"So I began with the hardest one: my Dad. He was reading the newspaper when I approached him."

"Dad . . ."

"Yes, what?" he asked without lowering the newspaper.

"Dad, I would like to talk with you."

"Well, talk."

"I mean. . . . It's really important."

The newspaper came down three slow inches. "What is it?"

"Dad, I love you. I just wanted you to

know that."

Tom smiled at me and said with obvious satisfaction, as though he felt a warm and secret joy flowing inside of him: "The newspaper fluttered to the floor. Then my father did two things I could never remember him ever doing before. He cried and he hugged me. And we talked all night, even though he had to go to work the next morning. It felt so good to be close to my father, to see his tears, to feel his hug, to hear him say that he loved me.

"It was easier with my mother and little brother. They cried with me, too, and we hugged each other, and started saying real nice things to each other. We shared the things we had been keeping secret for so many years. I was only sorry about one thing: that I had waited so long. Here I was, in the shadow of death, and I was just beginning to open up to all the people I had actually been close to.

"Then, one day I turned around and God was there. He didn't come to me when I pleaded with him. I guess I was like an animal trainer holding out a hoop. 'C'mon, jump through. C'mon, I'll give you three days . . . three weeks.' Apparently God does things in his own way and at his own hour.

"But the important thing is that he was there. He found me. You were right. He found me even after I stopped looking for him."

"Tommy," I practically gasped, "I

> think you are saying something very important and much more universal than you realize. To me, at least, you are saying that the surest way to find God is not to make him a private possession, a problem solver, or an instant consolation in time of need, but rather by opening to love. You know, St. John said that. He said 'God is love, and anyone who lives in love is living with God and God is living in him.' "[6]

Relationships—they can be so hurtful, so destructive. But they can be life-giving too, when touched with the love of God.

Notes

1. John Powell, S.J., *Unconditional Love* (Niles, IL: Argus Communications, 1978). p. 69.
2. Ibid., p. 56.
3. Sharon Johnson, from an unpublished manuscript © 1981 by Sharon Johnson.
4. John Powell, S.J., *Fully Human, Fully Alive* (Niles, IL: Argus Communications, 1976), pp. 150,151.
5. Wayne W. Dyer, *Pulling Your Own Strings* (New York: Thomas Y. Crowell Co., 1978), pp. 126,127.
6. Powell, *Unconditional Love*, pp. 110-116.

PART V
Your Performance Counts

Chapter 14

Achievement Is for Everyone, Isn't It?

How would you respond to the following agree/disagree statement? "Self-esteem should be based entirely on *being* or identity and not at all on behavior or performance."

Perhaps you aren't sure you understand the statement clearly enough to agree or disagree. The following passage spells out much the same proposition. See whether or not you agree with it.

> Most important, do I feel bad because I haven't accomplished enough? Achieved enough? Conformed enough? This is blackmail and antithetical to my philosophy. I must fight to give myself the right to feel good about myself and to feel good mood-wise, regardless of any accomplishment or nonaccomplishment whatsoever.[1]

I have heard leading Christian speakers say much the same thing. I have read it in the writings of various authors. Personally, I must disagree, however, though I understand why it is said and I sympathize with the intent.

I believe the statement expresses serious error, despite the fact that a correct concept underlies it. It is correct that we are of value apart from anything we might do. We have essential worth as human beings. From the Christian perspective, we are of value as children of God and saints, as we discussed in chapter 7. However, this concept is carried too far when the claim is made or the impression is given that our performance should not affect our self-esteem at all.

Perhaps we have stumbled onto one reason self-esteem teachings sometimes don't take. Counselors tell people their performance doesn't count, but though the people want to believe that, a more convincing voice inside them says it does count. That voice is not simply the misguided teachings of their parents or the culture. It is, I believe, a voice from God.

The very first thing God ever said to man was, "Be fruitful and increase in number; fill the earth and subdue it. Rule over . . . every living creature that moves on the ground" (Gen. 1:28).

This command identifies two of the most basic functions of man. The first is to reproduce (be fruitful, increase in number, fill the earth). The second is to achieve control and to exercise control over the earth.

Clearly the first function relates to each of us personally and directly. We are sexual beings, and coming to terms with our sexuality in a positive, constructive way is essential to our well-being.

The second function relates to us in a similar fashion. We are achiever/manager beings. We need to be gaining control and exercising control over

God's creation (see Ps. 8:3-8; Heb. 2:5-9).

When the Bible commands us to subdue and rule, it makes only one major exception. We are not to try to dominate other people. Jesus was emphatic about that. He said: "You know that the rulers of the Gentiles lord it over them, and their high officials exercise authority over them. Not so with you. Instead, whoever wants to become great among you must be your servant" (Matt. 20:25,26).

This crucial teaching of Jesus means that the divine mandate to subdue and rule cannot include our dominating one another. Therefore, the tactics recommended in *Winning Through Intimidation* by Robert Ringer are inappropriate for the Christian, except as one needs to know them to ward off the intimidators.

Significantly, though, in the above quoted passage, Jesus did not speak against wanting to "become great" when it's by serving people rather than using them. Self-realization is one thing, while dominating, using, intimidating, or exploiting people is quite another.

Psychologists talk about various kinds of behavior as different "social motivations," though their lists vary somewhat and so do their definitions of each motive. The desire to subdue and rule the creature universe, I identify with achievement motivation. The desire to dominate other people is a form of power motivation gone sour.

To return to our original agree/disagree statement, I maintain that we have an inner need to achieve because we were designed by God to be achievers. Therefore, we are not going to feel good about ourselves if we lack this essential component in our lives.

The Nonproductive Life

Jesus' parable of the barren fig tree has something to say to us on the question of performance. "A man had a fig tree, planted in his vineyard, and he went to look for fruit on it, but did not find any. So he said to the man who took care of the vineyard, 'For three years now I've been coming to look for fruit on this fig tree and haven't found any. Cut it down! Why should it use up the soil?'

" 'Sir,' the man replied, 'leave it alone for one more year, and I'll dig around it and fertilize it. If it bears fruit next year, fine! If not, then cut it down' " (Luke 13:6-9).

You and I are planted in God's vineyard taking up space, and He expects some "fruit" from us. Otherwise, why should He leave us here?

By contrast, Dr. Wayne Dyer writes:

> You exist. You are human. That is all you need. Your worth is determined by you, and with no need for an explanation to anyone. And your worthiness, a given, has nothing to do with your behavior and feelings.[2]

There it is again. Performance is totally disallowed as affecting worth. But from a biblical viewpoint, it is *not* enough that you exist, that you are human. As the psalmist writes: "Know that the Lord is God. It is he who made us, and we are his, we are his people, the sheep of his pasture" (Ps. 100:3).

We are His people. He has a right to expect some return from us—and He does expect some return. Just what the "fruit" should be is another question. We don't all have to attain great things as men count greatness. Praise is fruit. Worship is fruit. But the principle remains: We are God's people living in God's world, and we need to be fruitful if we are to live at peace with ourselves and with Him.

Let's be clear what we mean by achievement when we say achievement is for everyone. We must not equate achievement with success, for . . .

Success Is Not Enough

A full-page ad in a major daily newspaper carries the bold headline: "The Lazy Man's Way to Riches." The copy proceeds to boast about how well off the man who placed the ad is. He owns boats, mansions, beach properties, Cadillacs, stocks and bonds. He has money in the bank and plenty of leisure time. The ad concludes, "A month from today, you can be nothing more than 30 days older—or you can be on your way to getting rich."

There is little kinship between a person who would grab for a "lazy man's way to riches" and an achiever. The ad virtually offers *success without achievement* and should be viewed with suspicion to say the least.

Scripture warns us that "people who want to get rich fall into temptation and a trap and into many foolish and harmful desires that plunge men into ruin and destruction. For the love of money is a root of all kinds of evil" (1 Tim. 6:9,10).

A tale is told of a young man encountering Satan. The two met on a hilltop early one morning. Satan, posing as a great benefactor, said, "Young man, I like you. I can see you have ambition and want to make the greatest possible success of your life. I want to help you. Look at this great land lying before us. I will give you, as a permanent possession, all of this land that you can cover by sundown tonight. But there is one condition: you must be back here by sundown, not one moment later."

The young man's heart leaped within him at the thought of such an opportunity, but he would be no fool. He must not try to encompass so much ground as to return late and forfeit everything. As he passed over the fertile lands and well-watered plains, he kept close track of the sun making its own circuit of the heavens. When it was directly overhead, he resolutely turned away from the land that alluringly beckoned him on and began the return leg of his journey.

All went well until the young man's steps took him past some springs bubbling from the ground, the stream flowing away into a sheltered cove just outside the area he was encompassing. *The perfect site for a home and fruit orchard,* he thought. *The one thing I'd need to make my holdings complete.* He looked at the sun still high in the afternoon sky, looked again at the Eden so close to being his, and altered his course.

The detour took longer than he expected, what with having to wade the stream. He'd need to hurry to make up the lost time. But he was weary now. It had been a long day and a very long journey. It hadn't even occurred to him that his strength might run out before his time did. He should have turned back before noon, he told himself; should have allowed longer for the return than for the journey out; should never have added that watercourse to his return trip.

He was struggling now, his feet heavy, his legs aching, his eyes watching, watching as the sun sank ever closer to the western horizon. And then at last he saw it. The hill! It loomed before him, and on top of it stood the waiting figure of his benefactor.

His body told him to give up, that it was impossible. If he were fresh, he could sprint, and he just might make it. But he was exhausted. Silencing the cries of his tortured flesh, he broke into a run. The ground flew beneath his feet, but the sun seemed almost to match his pace in its plunge from the sky. *Faster, faster,* he ordered. His heart pounded furiously against his chest and his circle of vision narrowed until only at the center was their light. Still he lurched forward until he collapsed finally at Satan's feet.

"Congratulations, young man, I see you've made it," Satan said as the edge of the burning red disc of the sun dropped from sight. But there was no response from the young man who lay crumpled at his feet. "You shall have exactly what I promised," said Satan, "all the land you cover by sundown as a permanent possession." Then he laughed fiendishly. "I'd say you cover just about six feet." And they buried the young man there.[3]

"People who want to get rich fall into . . . a trap" (1 Tim. 6:9). That's one problem with "success motivation." It so easily translates into greed or vainglory. That's why I'm writing about achievement rather than about success. A person who aims at success is focused on the wrong thing, especially if his idea of success is to get rich.

Getting Things Done

One of the leading authorities in the study of achievement motivation is David C. McClelland, a Harvard psychologist. After reading others' reports of his work and after reading his book *The Achieving Society,* I telephoned McClelland personally to inquire about his views.

"Many people misunderstand what I mean by achievement," he told me. "Don't equate achievement motivation with success motivation. What I'm talking about might be called efficiency."

Later I found a similar definition in his book *Power, the Inner Experience,* in which he writes of achievement as "the satisfaction of doing a job well or efficiently, whether anyone else knows about it our not."

Exactly. Achievement relates to getting things done. Achievement is actual accomplishment, while success is an incidental result that sometimes follows.

You see, if a person does something—anything—particularly well, he is likely to gain money and recognition because of it. "Do you see a man skilled in his work? He will serve before kings; he will not serve before obscure men" (Prov. 22:29). His real credit, however, is in what he does, not in the success he enjoys as a result.

This is not to suggest that the achiever is totally indifferent to success. In most cases he'd like it very much if his efforts were rewarded. Partly he likes money and recognition because they are pleasant to have, and partly he likes them because they are tangible evidences that he indeed is achieving something worthwhile. But his focus is on the achieving, not on the reward.

What we are saying, then, is this: success may or may not be God's will for you, but achievement certainly is. Achieving is not optional. It isn't for the highly motivated only. It isn't the private concern of those who are into some human potential or success movement.

Achievement is for you.

God made you that way.

If all we've said so far hasn't established that fact, the direct command of the New Testament should. I refer to Titus 3:14—"Our people must learn to devote themselves to doing what is good, in order that they may provide for daily necessities and not live unproductive lives."

As a Christian living in today's society you have a concern that goes beyond simply providing our daily necessities. Welfare might do that. Begging might do it. Your concern is to lead a productive life—to get something worthwhile done.

The mischief in linking self-esteem with achievement comes when we fall into the trap of comparing our achievements with those of someone else. That is what is damaging and misguided.

Two years ago, after pondering these matters for some time, I crystallized in writing what I believed on the subject. The conclusions still wear well, so I share them with you now:

> As a person, I am unique. Therefore, my worth is not based or even related to some comparison of me with others. We both may be humans, both male, both writers, and so on, but only one of us is *me*. Therefore, the only appropriate comparison possible is between a better and worse me.

My achievement has nothing to do with your achievement. What may be a snap for you may be a real attainment for me. But while I do not need to match you, I do need my own sense of attainment.

As the Scripture says, "Each one should test his own actions. Then he can take pride in himself, without comparing himself to somebody else" (Gal. 6:4).

Yes, achievement is for everyone.

Notes

1. Dr. Theodore Isaac Rubin, *Compassion and Self-Hate* (New York: David McKay Co., 1975), p. 183.
2. Wayne W. Dyer, *Your Erroneous Zones* (New York: Thomas Y. Crowell Co., 1976), p. 43.
3. Adapted from Leo Tolstoy, "How Much Land Does a Man Need?"

Chapter 15

Encouraging Achievement in Yourself and Others

How does one grow an achiever? If you want to make your life count but lack drive, can you do anything about it? If you want your children to be doers, actively seeking productive lives, is there any way you can encourage that?

To seek answers we could examine the lives of individuals who have achieved much and try to figure out what made them tick. The trouble is we would have little idea how much their achievement depended on motivational principles we observe and how much it resulted from their own unique combination of gifts and opportunities.

There is another approach. We can look at some great societies. When a people as a whole register impressive achievement, it seems pretty clear they must be doing something right.

What Made Them Great?

Many theories have been advanced to explain the rise and fall of great societies. Unfortunately,

Christians have sometimes been preoccupied with the decline and fall side of the ledger. We see what happened to the Roman Empire or to the cities of Sodom and Gomorrah, and we warn of dangerous parallels in our own culture. As valid as that may be it can produce a decline-and-fall mentality. Instead of producing anything positive we get caught up in forever trying to slow the processes of degeneration. We become mere reactors to existing conditions instead of initiators of good. That's not a desirable pattern for us when we speak in the name of the Creator.

Before ever a society declined and fell it first had to rise. We should ask what made it rise. One sometimes popular theory for explaining the rise of a great culture is basically racist. For example, blacks supposedly could never build a great civilization because they were slave-caliber people, and regardless of their social or legal status that was all one could ever expect of them.

The racist view of societies has taken many novel forms. Some have been sinister and murderous, like Hitler's. He was ready to kill millions of Jews and other "inferiors" in the interests of an Aryan super race.

Other forms of racism have seemingly been innocuous—like the claim that Nordic people have influenced the rise of most great civilizations. Then there are the amusing variations such as Fanfani's claim that people with long heads make the best businessmen.

Since we can do nothing about our racial origins, and little about the shape of our heads, these theories seem more useful for giving people excuses than anything else. They give the unmotivated an excuse to stagnate and the exploiters an excuse to ride over others.

Another widely-held view, best advanced by the Yale geographer Ellsworth Huntington, is that climate determines the vigor and greatness of a society. In his book *Civilization and Climate*, published in 1915, Huntington pointed out that no great civilization has ever flourished in either the arctic zones or the tropics. Presumably survival is such a struggle in frigid climates that the people have little time for anything more. In the tropics, it's just too hot to think or work very much.

Huntington plotted in detail the exact temperature variations needed for optimum human development and the areas of the globe where such a climate prevails. If you think he was right, you may want to move your place of residence accordingly.

However, while climate can no doubt encourage or limit achievement, it seems clear that it cannot cause it. After all, the nations in Huntington's ideal climates vary widely in achievement. For that matter, a single nation may change greatly over a relatively short period of time while its climate remains the same. Obviously something more than climate is involved. I believe the one major factor is psychological.

Whether you want to change your place of residence or not, you might try changing your attitude. That sounds so simple, though not always so easy. Is there any hard evidence that it would do any good? Yes there is.

Substantial historical evidence supports the view that achievement does not depend so much on various fortuitous circumstances as on psychological orientation. In other words, *people who want to achieve and who think of themselves as achievers really do get things done.*

David C. McClelland's (see previous chapter) studies of great societies past and present indicate that *before* a given culture reached its peak, achievement motivation was high. For example, for 200 years before the Golden Age of Pericles—the fifth century B.C., when Athenian culture was at its peak and the wonders of the Acropolis were built—achievement themes were prominent in the speeches, orations, dramas, poems, and other literature. By the time the culture reached its zenith, achievement motivation had gone into decline, and the culture soon followed.

This pattern appears not only in ancient Athens but in contemporary cultures worldwide. The rise and fall of motivation *precedes* the rise and fall of achievement.

All of this should come as good news to us because it means that we can accomplish things too once we find ways to turn on our "want to."

Now we come to the real issue. What specific, practical actions can a person take to stimulate a desire to achieve, in himself or others? I suggest four possibilities.

1. *To develop achievement motivation, one should read extensively in achievement-oriented literature.* It matters what we read. If I didn't believe that, I wouldn't waste my time writing. I believe this book can and will change lives. I know my own life has been influenced, sometimes decisively, by what I have read.

I'm not suggesting, however, that you concentrate your reading on popular psychology or self-help books. Other contemporary literature rich in achievement motivation ranges from delightful children's stories such as *The Little Engine That*

Could and *Abel's Island* to the biographies of George Washington Carver and Helen Keller. From *Profiles in Courage* to *Roots* to *The Incredible Journey*.

I am concerned, however, with what a comparison of our present literary and television/movie diet with that of a generation ago might show. I would guess we'd see a frightening decline in the achievement content. The old-time hero who prevailed against overwhelming odds has in many cases been replaced by a somewhat dissolute, easygoing character who is the victim of a corrupt system.

Fortunately, one great source of achievement-oriented reading—the source that probably most influenced achievers of the past and present—is still available to us. I refer to the Bible. What towering examples of achievement in the face of adversity we find there! We read—

—of Noah, who built a great lifeboat though he had to work for 120 years under the derisive gaze of his contemporaries to do it;

—of Abraham, who left the security of Ur to pioneer and to claim an uncharted wilderness;

—of Joseph, a forgotten man in prison in a foreign land, who rose to become governor of that land;

—of Moses, who defied the wrath of Pharaoh, and led an army of malcontents through a 40-year trek in the wilderness to make of them a nation;

—of Gideon, the "loaf of barley bread," who routed an army of 135,000 men with a band of 300;

—of the tragic Samson, who killed more enemies of the Lord at his death than he did during his lifetime;

—of David, venturing out against the fearful giant Goliath and returning the victor;

—of Daniel, coming out of a den of lions—alive—with the result that a pagan king proclaimed the God of Daniel to be supreme over all.

When Scripture lists the greatest heroes of all time, it talks largely of achievement, of those who "through faith conquered kingdoms, administered justice, and gained what was promised; who shut the mouths of lions, quenched the fury of the flames, and escaped the edge of the sword; whose weakness was turned to strength; and who became powerful in battle and routed foreign armies" (Heb. 11:33,34).

Jesus Himself is presented in Scripture as a man with a goal to achieve. He told His disciples, "My food . . . is to do the will of him who sent me and to finish his work" (John 4:34). Another time He said, "I have a baptism to undergo, and how distressed I am until it is completed!" (Luke 12:50).

The writer to the Hebrews says that Jesus "for the joy set before him endured the cross, scorning its shame, and sat down at the right hand of the throne of God" (Heb. 12:2). I would not trivialize His great sacrifice by comparing it with our ventures. His is the all-surpassing Achievement. Yet we, like our Lord, will endure whatever it takes to achieve our ends if the joy of doing so is set vividly before us.

One way to set the joy of achievement before us is to read of others' triumphs. Yes, if you want to become an achiever, read achievement-oriented literature. Read the Bible. Doing so could be one reason so many people with evangelical roots have excelled in all walks of life.

2. *To become an achiever, affiliate with a church that encourages independent devotion and personal responsibility before God.* McClelland writes:

> It may be concluded with reasonable confidence that, as of 1950, Protestant countries are economically more advanced on the average, even taking their differences in natural resources into account, than are Catholic countries.[1]

There appears to be a consistent pattern historically for members of certain Protestant sects (Quakers, Anabaptists, Methodists) to show remarkable enterprise. All of these sects in their early days were "ultra-protestant" in the sense of strongly rejecting traditional church authority and stressing the individual's direct communion with God.

One might ask whether this religious individualism really produced achievers or whether the two traits just happened to coincide. Striking evidence that the former is the case comes from the other great religions of the world.

Among the Hindus of north India, for example, it is the small Vaishnava sect—which claims that worship by lay people in their homes is as valid as worship led by a priest in the temple—that is conspicuously successful in business compared to other Hindus. McClelland writes:

> The number of similar cases could be multiplied: the rise of the business class in Japan in the 19th century was associated with a special form of Buddhism—Zen, which again is a form of positive mysticism which is definitely individual-

istic and against many ritual forms.[2]

As one last example, McClelland cites the Jews:

> It is a curious fact that the distinct business success of Jews within the past few generations has been associated with a strong antirabbinical mystical movement within Judaism known as Hassidism . . . an attempt to escape from "formalism and ecclesiastical systems" and to encourage the believer to feel that he could directly and joyously feel the presence of God.[3]

In an interesting test of his theories, McClelland matched two Mexican villages, one a traditional Catholic village and one that had been converted to Protestantism. He found that the Protestants were generally higher in achievement motivation than were their Catholic counterparts. (He also found a much wider variation among the Protestants: they had a few individuals who tested highest and a few who tested lowest.)

Today one certainly cannot assume that every fellowship of Protestants will encourage individualism and that every Catholic church will be tradition-bound. What one can assume is that any church, whatever its label, that exalts formal, ritualistic religion above a direct, personal relationship with God does so to the detriment of its members' achievement motivation. To say nothing of their spiritual welfare.

3. *To help your children become achievers, encourage self-reliance in them at an early age.* What characterizes the relationships between parents and their children in homes that produce the highest achievers? Researchers have sought answers to that question.

Marian R. Winterbottom, and many others after her, found that a mother's attitude in bringing up her children has a significant effect on their achievement motivation. Winterbottom sought to determine at what ages children were expected to learn self-reliance in such matters as—

—feeding themselves without help;
—undressing and preparing for bed;
—taking care of toys and clothes;
—doing assigned household chores;
—playing in the neighborhood outside their yards;
—making their own friends;
—deciding how to spend their own money;
—entertaining themselves;
—doing well in competition.

Winterbottom discovered that sons whose mothers expected self-reliance of them at relatively early ages rated high in achievement motivation. Those sons kept dependent on their parents characteristically were less interested in achievement.

Subsequent testing by other researchers supported these conclusions but with some significant modifications. It seems that the *reason* a mother demands self-reliance in her children is important. If she "abandons" the child to care for himself so that she won't have to be bothered or because she is simply careless and indifferent, no positive effect on the child's desire for achievement follows. The mother needs to be warmly involved with her children, supporting them and praising their accomplishments. She also needs to be a person of reasonably high standards and expectations herself.

A father can also have a significant effect on his child's achievement motivation. Dominating fathers who tell their children exactly what to do and how to do it rather than letting them function on their own with only minimum necessary guidance tend to produce underachievers. This may explain why strong fathers so often produce weak sons.

That pattern is not unavoidable. Many strong fathers are good and wise enough to give their children room to grow. Others may be so busily occupied with their own exploits that their children escape their close supervision. In either case the child may do well, though in the one case it is because of the father's virtues and in the other despite his neglect. Anyhow, the strong father who is closely involved with his children needs to be careful not to dominate them, because his natural instincts will no doubt run that way.

Scripture says, "It is good for a man to bear the yoke while he is young" (Lam. 3:27). That seems to be another way of saying: train your children early in self-reliance.

4. *To become an achiever despite any disadvantages from your past, repent and believe the Scriptures*. Your parents may not have encouraged self-reliance in you at an early age. Your church background may not have been stimulating to your individual initiative. You may not have been raised on a diet of stories of great achievers. As a result, you may be disadvantaged but *you are not disqualified*.

No one has an ideal background. That's why we all need the grace of God. We live in a fallen world. Our parents and others who have influenced our lives are all imperfect. It would be foolish to argue that undesirable influences have had no effect on us. They have. But what we become does not have to be determined by these powerful forces from the past. The grace of God can make a difference. God the Creator can work creatively in us. And He will, as we trust Him to do so.

First, though, a person must clarify his concept of what he should do and be. How can you ask God to change your life in this or that respect if you don't know what changes are needed?

We've now come full circle in this section. In chapter 14 we cited the command of God to subdue and rule the earth. We said that means each of us should become an achiever. Jesus had something to say on the same subject, and He said it in the form of a parable.

> "A man going on a journey . . . called his servants and entrusted his property to them. To one he gave five talents of money, to another two talents, and to another one talent, each according to his ability. Then he went on his journey. The man who had received the five talents went at once and put his money to work and gained five more. So also, the one with the two talents gained two more. But the man who had received the one talent went off, dug a hole in the ground and hid his master's money.
>
> "After a long time the master of those servants returned and settled accounts with them. The man who had received the five talents brought the other five. 'Master,' he said, 'you entrusted me with five talents. See, I have gained five more.'
>
> "His master replied, 'Well done, good and faithful servant! You have been faithful with a few things; I will put you in

charge of many things. Come and share your master's happiness!'

"The man with the two talents also came. 'Master,' he said, 'you entrusted me with two talents; see, I have gained two more.'

"His master replied, 'Well done, good and faithful servant! You have been faithful with a few things; I will put you in charge of many things. Come and share your master's happiness!'

Then the man who had received the one talent came. 'Master,' he said, 'I knew that you are a hard man, harvesting where you have not sown and gathering where you have not scattered seed. So I was afraid and went out and hid your talent in the ground. See, here is what belongs to you.'

"His master replied, 'You wicked, lazy servant! So you knew that I harvest where I have not sown and gather where I have not scattered seed? Well then, you should have put my money on deposit with the bankers, so that when I returned I would have received it back with interest' " (Matt. 25:14-27).

Notice that the parable describes the ways in which three different people use the resources entrusted to them. Two invest their money, double it, and receive commendation and increased opportunity. The third person buries his and seems to argue that he has done well to break even. For this, he is severely reprimanded.

An important question to ask is, What motivated the third man? He said, "I was afraid, and went out and hid your talent" (v. 25).

I was afraid. Certainly one of the chief enemies of achievement is fear of failure. Ironically, the man who feared failure in the parable is the only one who experienced it. You see, fear of failure does nothing to lessen the likelihood of failure and in fact tends to assure it by incapacitating a person. If you are paralyzed by fear or struggling with it, read the previous section of this book again, and especially chapter 11.

But why was the man in the parable afraid? He said to his master, "I knew that you are a hard man, harvesting where you have not sown . . . so I was afraid" (vv. 24,25).

Wasn't that irrational? If the master were so adept at making everything turn a profit, why did not this man, in effect a partner of the master, expect happy results? Apparently he saw himself more as a potential victim of the master than as a partner.

This man represents the person who has a basically negative view of God and the world. God is a "hard man," and this world He has placed us in eats up its inhabitants. One does well to hold his own in this fearful place, let alone gain anything. And God is a rigorous Judge who will not brook any failure.

So then, the fear of the non-achiever betrays the fact that he has a spiritual problem. Thus, the master says, "You wicked, lazy servant!" (v. 26). In the master's judgment, this man's inactivity reveals a moral flaw, not just an unfortunate choice. The man was *wicked.*

Now that is interesting. When was the last time you heard a sermon on the wickedness of not developing your achievement potential? Preachers have called many things sinful—too often things that the Bible never so designates—but too few call wicked this dereliction of duty that the Lord so clearly condemns.

Even though you may not hear this preached much, it is by no means a novel idea. Sloth traditionally has been recognized by the church as one of the seven deadly sins. That's why this fourth principle for encouraging achievement motivation is *repent and believe the Scriptures*. God can certainly give you grace to accomplish many worthwhile things during your lifetime, but first you must realize He expects you to do exactly that.

Now it's your move.

Get started, and God will be with you.

Say, did you notice what was *missing* from the parable? We saw servants who set out to accomplish something and did. We saw a servant who held back and was condemned. But we didn't see anyone who ventured out and failed.

How come?

Because there is no such thing.

No such thing as venturing out and failing? That certainly cannot be true.

Right. What we're saying is that anyone who consistently seeks to develop and use his potential will not fail in the long run. Some of his projects may fail, but *he* won't. Furthermore, his failures will be only preliminary to the ultimate achievement of worthwhile goals.

One of my favorite Scriptures puts it this way. "Sow your seed in the morning, and at evening let not your hands be idle, for you do not know which will succeed, whether this or that, or whether both will do equally well" (Eccl. 11:6).

Note the possibilities. Maybe morning sowing

will succeed. Maybe evening sowing. Maybe both. What is not mentioned? *Maybe neither.*

Like Jesus' parable of the talents, this verse allows for no such thing as ultimate failure for the consistent sower. So seize your opportunities. You don't know which of your efforts will bear fruit, but some will. You may be happily surprised to find some day that they all did.

Notes

1. D.C. McClelland, *The Achieving Society* (Princeton: D. Van Nostrand Co., 1961), p. 53.
2. Ibid., p. 369.
3. Ibid., p. 370.

Stanley C. Baldwin offers seminars and meetings teaching these principles to churches and groups across the United States and Canada. If you would like to know when he will be in your area, or if you want information on scheduling a seminar, write:

Truth for Our Times
P.O. Box 101
Oregon City, Oregon 97045